BLOCK SALT
And
CANDLES

To the memory of my parents;
to all Trehafod people, past, present and future;
and for Michael, Richard and Sarah, who love the place.

BLOCK SALT
And
CANDLES

A Rhondda Childhood

Mary Davies Parnell

SEREN BOOKS

Seren Books

Seren Books is the book imprint of
Poetry Wales Press Ltd
Andmar House, Tondu Road, Bridgend
Mid-Glamorgan

© Mary Davies Parnell, 1991

British Library Cataloguing in Publication Data
for this title is available from the British Library Data Office.

ISBN: 1-85411-056-X

*The publisher acknowledges the financial support of the
Rhondda Borough Council and The Welsh Arts Council.*

Cover Illustration — Tom Hutchinson

Typeset in Plantin by SB Datagraphics, Colchester.
Printed in Wales by WBC, Bridgend.

CONTENTS

List of Illustrations

1. Author, (c. 1941)
2. Author, (c. 1941)
3. Paternal Grandparents, father
4. Jack, 1935
5. St. Barnabas' Church and shop
6. Sal, (c.1935)
7. Painting of Tydraw, 1979
8. Tydraw, kitchen entrance, 1940s
9. Tydraw, steps to loft, 1940s
10. Standard 4, Hafod School
11. Trehafod children, 1965
12. Lewis Merthyr Colliery
13. Upper Trehafod
14. Infants Sunday School class
15. Lewis Merthyr Colliery, 1960s
16. The river Rhondda Fawr
17. The author, aged 8
18. Church Programme

Foreword

The infinite pleasure I derived from reading this book makes it a privilege and honour to write a foreword.

Mary Davies Parnell is to be congratulated on her total recall of her young life, which encapsulates the humour, problems and intimate details which typify an ordinary, loving, mining valley family.

Her personal experiences inject a warm, sincere and sympathetic depth to her writing which makes it compulsive reading and which will suit every age group, covering the historical, educational and nostalgic aspects of our beloved Rhondda.

I am sure it will achieve international acclaim and I wish it every success.

Hon. Freeman Councillor Mattie Collins, MBE
Leader, Rhondda Borough Council.

Preface

One March evening of last year we were sitting quietly, drinking a cup of coffee and watching the best television programme of the week, when suddenly there was a small, apologetic bang — more of a plop, really — and everything went black. North Cardiff was experiencing a rare power failure. Torches and matches were fumbled for and a candle in a blue enamelled Wee Willie Winkie candle-holder fetched from the garage by my husband who is the spirit of organisation and methodical sense in such emergencies. The candles were relics of my father's shop in Trehafod, closed in 1977. After we had helped to enlighten our Japanese next-door neighbours, we settled down to finish our lukewarm coffee in the cosy gloom. The atmosphere took me back to my childhood. We had no lighting at all upstairs in the Trehafod house and in the 40s I tramped up the stairs to Bedfordshire' every evening, my way lit by a candle in that same holder. Our old neighbour did the same, but used to forget to douse the flame and weirdly and wonderfully ended up the next morning without any teeth!

Reminiscences began, stories were related and it was decided I should write them down... *Block Salt and Candles* is a collection of semi-autobiographical memories of growing up in Trehafod, Rhondda, during the years 1940 to 1948, with brief incursions into the 30s when my parents first met.

My thanks to South Wales Electricity for providing the power cut in the first place... Heartfelt thanks to Dr Glyn Jones and his wife, Doreen, who were the first outside my immediate family to read the typescript and give me encouragement; to my late cousin, Gwilym Mann, who provided me with a lot of historical information about Tydraw and the family and who patiently answered my questions and sought answers when he didn't know them; to my colleagues: Mrs Margaret Smith who supplied me with information about collieries and coal, and Mrs Gaynor Hurley who corrected my Welsh version of 'Pwsi Meri Mew' and translated it for me; to Meic Stephens who knows everything there is to know about Wales and told me the date of the Tynewydd pit disaster; to Mrs Doreen Lendrum who helped me with the Trehafod street names; to the Rhondda Borough council for their friendliness and financial help in publication and launch of the book, and especially their Leader, Honorary Freeman Mrs Mattie Collins, MBE, for her kind Foreword; and to Cary Archard, Mick Felton and Amy Wack of Seren Books who have ensured the book sees the light of day. Above all, my thanks and love to my husband, Michael, who started me off on the project, typed up my manuscript, sorted out my unrelated participles, wrongly corrected my spelling (though he was right once), word-processed the lot and is still my husband.

Mary Davies Parnell
Cardiff, January 1991

CHAPTER ONE

Granny Thomas

Granny Thomas was always burning her teeth. It seemed to me her face was different every week. In those pre-electricity days when only gas lights were available, and those downstairs, Granny Thomas needed a candle to light her way to her bed. She would take what was left of the day's newspaper, the *Daily Herald,* after her grandson had torn out photos of footballers and her daughter had kept the farming or the economy pages to light tomorrow's fire, and read it in bed. When her octogenarian eyes wearied, she would take out her set of false teeth, put them on the candlestick and turn over to go to sleep, forgetting to extinguish the flame. Then all that was left when she reached for her teeth next morning ready to put them in her mouth and apply them to her breakfast was a pile of grey ashes.

At my wondering why people furnished with false teeth needed to take them out at night or at all, my mother would say, "Well, just in case we swallow them, Mari fach. Anyway, they're uncomfortable when you're sleeping."

I didn't quite understand the logicality of the latter statement, and to someone who has difficulty in swallowing an aspirin without the thing dissolving into a soggy, gritty, foul-tasting mess in the mouth, the former observation troubled my mind too. Swallowing a set of teeth, especially in sleep, appeared a feat even more remarkable than the mini-bonfire. And why didn't the smell of burning wake old Granny Thomas and warn her that yet another set was going up in flames? No doubt she was peacefully and deeply asleep, practising for her eternal slumbers.

She didn't seem to care about being toothless for most of her elderly life. They ate a lot of sop in that house anyway and her favourite snack was a buttered cream cracker softened in tea. She would come into our corner shop and say to my mother with what seemed to me a wicked grin, "I've burnt my teeth again, Mrs Davies. Never mind, the bottom ones did pinch a bit on the side! Can I have a packet of cream crackers, please? I'll pay you tomorrow." Then, clutching her purchase, off she would go to the front room with the sloping floor which was her domain in the Thomas house two doors further up the street.

The cream crackers didn't last long, for they were also given to the village children as rewards for running her not infrequent errands. "Tommy 'Awkins, run down to the post office for a penny stamp for me, will you? There's a good boy. I'll give you a nice cream cracker when you come back." A frowning, reluctant but unprotesting Tommy would slowly disappear from sight down Church Hill, sullenly and muttering to himself, kicking loose stones, to return perhaps an hour later, for it was a fair old walk. He would as promised be rewarded with another "There's a good boy you are, Tommy 'Awkins" and a buttered cream cracker.

When Granny Thomas put her round, smiling, pasty face outside the door, with mouth sunken in when the previous night's activities had ended in conflagration, the kids would vanish off the street in seconds.

I was a frequent visitor to the Thomas' house as one of her grandsons, David, was the child nearest in age and address if not sex to me and he was my playmate. He had developed a knack of disappearing when his granny needed a stamp. This was easy when you lived in the same house, as she had a habit of talking to herself, so he knew in advance of impending errands and took appropriate evading action. Sometimes, going to call for him to play, I would see him haring towards and past me, disappearing round the corner without stopping for a word of explanation, and *I* would be caught to fetch two eggs from Terry Stores for Granny Thomas.

Although we had a wireless, at one point during the war the battery that was a vital part of its innards went permanently flat; no sound could be persuaded out of the radio other than a colicky rattle, and no replacement battery could be found anywhere in the vicinity. My mother couldn't live without the News, so nightly at six p.m. I was despatched to the Thomas household to listen to Frank Phillips, Alvar Liddell or Joseph McLeod reading the current account of the state of the war and report back to my parents. I mostly found this a very boring job and kept forgetting to listen, especially if something interesting was going on at the same time, such as David feeding jelly to the canary or putting his socks on the cat. As a result my parents had an unreliable but optimistic account of the progress of the war as I made up things I thought would please them.

"Anything much happen today, Mary?"

"Oh, yes. The British have captured another bridge."

"Oh. Where?"

"Oh" (desperately thinking) "— um — in Berlin, I think they said."

"Berlin!? Don't be so silly. The British army are nowhere near Berlin!"

"Oh, well, somewhere beginning with a B."

"Hm. Any casualties?"

"No. No British soldiers killed today. Only Germans. And we've captured ten tanks somewhere." It was a good job the *Western Mail* would put them right, giving them accurate if sometimes disappointing news the next day.

Granny Thomas's front room floor sloped down towards the fireplace from the door opposite, not because of the heavy iron grate at one end but because this was Trehafod, Rhondda, a coal-mining village where all the floors sloped and the houses often stood at crazy angles to each other, even the terraced ones. My father once told me that the coal landlord had built his house, 'Hafod Fawr', high above the valley floor on the hillside where there was a solid rock foundation of pennant sandstone and no fear of subsidence. He also had a good view of the colliery and the state of the work there.

"We, of course, are living on a hollow crust — a mere shell," my father would muse, as though we were doomed and about to disappear through a crack in the earth's surface into a vast cavern from which every scrap of coal had been excavated, en route the quick way to Australia.

Personally I thought what a terrible nuisance it would be to live in the big, grand house high on the opposite hillside, far away from the bus-stop, church, village, friends and above all the marvellous mountain on our side of the Rhondda river.

13

CHAPTER TWO

The Mountain

Trehafod, especially the Tump which is the upper part of the village overlooking the valley floor and basically composed of three terraces (Bryn Eirw, Woodfield and Rheolau, or Bottom, Second and Top Streets to the locals), may not be much to look at but was a paradise for children growing up. When in my teens and a Porth County 'snob' (as opposed to a Porth Secondary 'sardine'), I occasionally went to tea with school friends from various parts of the Rhondda Valleys, Fach and Fawr, but nowhere possessed a mountain half as exciting as Trehafod's.

Thanks to the Lewis Merthyr colliery, the bowels of the earth had been deposited at intervals from the valley bottom right to the very mountain top, some eight hundred feet higher, covering in neat mounds the sandstone, limestone and millstone grit of which the South Wales coalfield is composed. Those at the bottom had greened over and it was difficult to see where mountain ended and bowel began. As the eye rose upward, though, it was to another world of dark, hostile, dusty shale where even sheep could not get a sure footing. Not that they wanted to, as only sparse, tough clumps of grass grew on these tips, and that with difficulty. This was a sombre, silent world, the only sound being that of circling hawks and other birds of prey waiting to pounce on a stray sheep with a broken leg and about to release its hold on life. Even the few men who worked up there rarely spoke, it seemed, as they carried out their tip maintenance work. Now and then a voice echoed eerily around.

Occasionally bold valley boys set off, grim-faced, silent and never alone, to climb to the Black Lake, said to lie beyond the topmost tip and in which, so it was said, all life — frogs, newts, and fish — was as black as the inhabitants of the deepest oceans.

14

"Where you going then, Billy Luckwell?"

"Mind your own business, Mary Davies."

"Aw, come on, mun, say!"

"Up the Black Lake, if you must know, but don't think you can come, 'cos you can't, see?"

"I don't want to in any case."

"Aw, don't tell yer fibs, you do."

"No, I don't, see, 'cos my mother wouldn't let me."

The verbal exchanges would continue until Billy and his friend were out of earshot, trudging off as if this was a journey they had to accomplish.

Witnessed a day or two later, strutting around the streets, they were looked on as heroes, as though they had trekked to the South Pole like Captain Scott or had scaled Kilimanjaro. To get a girl's attention in Trehafod, all a lad had to do was set off for the Black Lake and be seen and heard doing it. I never knew of any girls who had ventured there or even cared to. For all we young ladies knew, it might have been a male myth.

The west-facing hillside opposite ours on the far side of the river was tamed. It had farms, the big house and a tarred road. Carts and an occasional car went along it. Old ladies went for walks there. It was a relatively uninteresting place, populated by adults. It was respectable, whereas our hillside was wild.

Above the Tump three feeder ponds filtered water down to the colliery. The top one, Coedcae, was fed by a mountain stream running from somewhere in the direction of Cymmer. This was the largest of the rectangular ponds where scores of dogs had been forced to learn to swim or drown, having been hurled in by their tough-minded owners. Thousands of minnows had been hauled from the pond, caught in jam jars which had been hurriedly and usually unthoroughly divested of their contents — Coedcae pond wild life had developed a sweet tooth! Brave men sometimes swam in its murky waters, and it was rumoured some had drowned, caught in the profuse, treacherous weeds in the middle, where there lurked, it was said, Coedcae's very own monster, a fish more than a foot in length, though no one had ever seen it for sure. Unwanted dogs in weighted sacks had met their maker there too, and many games of ducks and drakes had visibly reduced the size of an adjoining mound of stones and pebbles.

Early one Sunday morning Olly Pugh, pigeon-fancier extraordinaire of Lower Trehafod, but a Tump original, was walking with his offspring around Coedcae when he espied what he thought was a partly submerged sleeper near the bank. "Funny, that's a wide log, aye," he said to himself, then to his dismay realised it was a man's body.

"Didn't know who he was, mind, but oh, we ran as fast as we could, aye, down to Alice Lewis's, 'cos she got a phone, see. And we rang up the police, and they come and took the man's body down the Coll'ery in a tram. Jew jew, I'm stiff today after that run, aye."

Doubtless they discovered who the man was — perhaps someone who had had too much to drink in the Vaughan's Arms, taking a short cut home over the mountain but cutting short his days in the process.

At the southern end of the pond water spilled over into a conduit to feed the unoriginally named, smaller Middle Pond, which in turn fed the smallest, Bottom Pond. These latter two ponds were far more homely and manageable than Coedcae. There were no reeds, weeds or frogspawn; the water usually lapped right up to the level grassy surround and was clearer. In hot weather during the summer, Middle or Bottom, depending on the water level, became decidedly murkier as Tump children made it their own private swimming pool. Foreigners from downtown Trehafod were definitely not allowed in, nor dared they show their faces. Surrounding dense ferns provided natural changing rooms and discarded sleepers from the nearby tram railway were used as diving boards.

Accidents occurred with annual regularity. The bold ones would dive head first into the murk and occasionally a head would make forcible contact with a submerged bit of pennant and its owner be knocked out. Once a swaggerer dived in, caught the sharp edge of a rock in flight and opened himself up from the nave to the chaps, dyeing the water pink in the process. At such times, after the unfortunate person had been given juvenile first-aid, or in the case of the slit stomach an ambulance summoned, swimmers would vanish from the scene for a few days, warned off by anxious mothers, to return, at first surreptitiously then brazenly defiant, at the next hot spell.

My own mother, reluctant to see me join the rabble bathing in the pond, would at first try to dissuade me by reasonable argument:

"Nice girls don't go bathing in old mountain ponds."

Then, aware of my downturned mouth and feeling my stubborn resolve:"Don't go pulling those jibs at me. Boys pee in those ponds. *Ach y fi*! You can catch nasty diseases from that, you know."

Then finally:

"Mary! You are not to go bathing in that pond!"

I was always "Mary" when naughty or difficult, and "Mari fach" when good.

So I would have to put my bathers on under my clothes and stuff a small towel up my cardigan, then slip out while my mother was busy with a customer in the shop.

So-called friends appeared to sense my mother's antagonism to my pond-bathing and would threaten to tell her if I didn't get them lollipops, gob-stoppers or licorice sticks from the shop. That was no problem, compared with the reintroducing of wet towel and bathers back into the house, not to mention their subsequent concealment, so I didn't worry too much about them.

During the rest of the year, the main attraction of the ponds was submarine races, the submarines being once again sodden sleepers which had formerly graced the incline. These were hurled in at one end, often taking their skinny launcher into the water with them, and the triumphant submarine was the one longest true to its name. Dripping wet small persons were often to be seen making their way shiveringly and apprehensively home, trailing spirogyra and other assorted weeds. Interested passers-by would say with relish to the unfortunate: "Oh, fallen in Coedcae pond, have you? You'll cop it from your Mam!"

One of the hazards encountered before reaching the ponds was crossing the incline or tramway. The last words children heard as they left their houses and headed for the mountain were: "You watch out for those trams. Don't you come back here injured, mind." The trams — small pram-like contraptions, usually about ten or a dozen linked together — took waste from the colliery to be jettisoned high up towards the sky on the most recent tip. As one little train was laboriously hauled up by cable, another came hurtling down, the trucks bouncing, pitching and swaying independently of each other in a clatter of wheels and links and chains. Alas, they never collided, despite hopeful cries of, "They're going to crash! Look, they're heading straight at each other!" There was a chicane where each unfailingly passed the other with a deafening roar, creating mini-earthquakes on the nearby land.

Tip maintenance men rode up perched on the shale in the trucks and waved to the watching children on the levées. They looked like inverted black and white minstrels with their white faces and coal-dust-ringed eyes. On the way down there was no time to wave as they clung on for dear life. Needless to say the bold boys would hitch lifts up to nowhere on unattended runs. Some must have been derailed now and then, probably through the wiles of village boys, the 'rebels' as my mother called them, as the mountain around was dotted with old rusting trams, marvellous playthings, some upturned, in which children made fern-clad dens, others upright and full of bright, orange water with oily iridescent streaks, wheels askew or missing altogether. The mountain was truly a haven of delight. There were former abandoned tramways, now steep-sided gullies with small streams, boggy floors and an amazing array of plants, wild flowers and crawling creatures. A rusty pipe spanned such a one and the daring would edge across from one side to the other in an awkward sitting position, giving many mothers extra patching work on trouser seats and occasionally causing a parent's puzzled look at a girl's underwear: "Mary, what on earth have you been doing with your knickers? Look, the bum is all orange."

Ferns abounded and it was a joy to find a courting couple to plague. The word went round: "There's lovers in the ferns!" This was usually greeted with a derisory "Aaaagh! Soppy dabs!" The naughty children would congregate to spy on them, advancing quietly from behind with a fair amount of giggling and "Sssssh's" and armed with sheep's droppings, which were in abundance, to lob at the unsuspecting and soon irate couple. "Aw, Christ, bloody kids! Aw, look, the little sods are throwing sheepshit at us. I'll bloody kill 'em I will when I catch 'em, the little buggers!"

I never learned the facts of life from roaming on the mountains. Voyeurism was out: torment was in. But it did enlarge my vocabulary in language I didn't come across at home, my father never going beyond a mild "Jesus!", always under his breath, and all the swearing my mother ever seemed to know was "Hell's bells!". And we were never caught, as we scattered in all directions, so the frustrated lover never knew whom to chase.

CHAPTER THREE

The Corner Shop

My parents kept the corner shop which my paternal grandmother, Anne, had established when the family returned, disillusioned, from the USA in a time of depression at the end of the nineteenth century. My grandfather was not well enough to work, suffering from the miners' disease, pneumoconiosis, and my tiny, tough grandmother determined the family should be independent, properly dressed and fed through her own efforts if not through those of her ailing husband. Cleverly she worked out the best spot to set herself up in trade in the one house on the Tump everyone had to pass to reach their own, and had some notices printed which said: "Corner Shop, Bryn Eirw, Trehafod. Prop. A. Davies. Purveyor of Fine Foods. Weekly Orders Made Up and Delivered. Horniman's Tea." Later on England's Glory matches replaced Horniman's tea as more generous advertisers.

My father, when aged thirteen, was the delivery man, and the delivery vehicle was a home-made hand-cart. As time wore on and my grandmother's leniency in allowing customers to pay tomorrow, and her efficiency and kindliness became known, so the mileage of my father's rounds increased. He received payment of two kinds, money and tobacco. Cancer was not linked with cigarettes then and my father smoked from a comparatively early age. He lived into his eighties but the evil weed undoubtedly robbed him of several years and caused him a painful death, his thin body burdened with an enlarged, malfunctioning liver and cancer crushing his lungs.

It was a front-room shop with an extended window in an ordinary end of terrace house. It stood at the top of Bryn Eirw Hill, which led down to the Vaughan's Arms bus stop to Porth. The Vaughan's Arms was opposite, but to me it was of greater importance as a bus stop than a pub. Fortunately for Andrew Vaughan, this was not the case for the vast majority of Trehafod's population, and Mr Vaughan had donated a seat placed halfway up Bryn Eirw Hill to help his more loyal customers home.

The shop was opposite little St Barnabas's Church, which stood (as it still does) at the top of a pile of rough stones and earth known as Church Hill. Our shop was known as 'Philly's' or 'the Corner Shop': "Johnnie, go down Philly's and ask Mrs Davies for a pint of vinegar in this jug. If you don't spill any, you can have the penny change to spend." Sometimes, to bolder, familiar people, we were 'down Jack's' (my father's name).

Aunties of friends in lower Trehafod might ask, "Who are you then?" and I would pipe up, "I'm from Philly's shop up the Tump". In my earlier years this caused a bit of an identity crisis as I didn't really know who I was: was I Mary Philly or Mary Davies? However, looking one day in the huge Welsh Bible with the metal clasp and seeing my grandfather's name, "John Davies, born Caerphilly, 1863" on the frontispiece page, I asked my mother if I should write my surname there as Philly or Davies. First I was informed that I was not to write my name there; and secondly, I was of course a Davies. And she explained the Caerphilly connection. So Philly's we were.

Nevertheless, clarification of my identity didn't prevent my telling them in the Prince of Wales Hospital in Cardiff, when receiving treatment for a broken arm, that I was Shirley Davies, being an admirer of a certain Miss Temple. Indetermination followed me to the village school. Moving up from the Infants' to the Primary department, a teacher to whom we were unknown was asking for our full names.

"Jennifer Jane Rees," said one.

"Sylvia Sampson," said another.

"Clive Humphrey Jacobs," said yet another.

This went on until the most glorious name assailed my ears: "Hilary Primrose Allen," said a pretty, dark-lashed and dark-haired, ringletted girl sitting nearby. This was far superior to Shirley Temple. Primrose! Thoughts of the pretty flowers in shady glades flitted through my mind, no doubt evoking more thoughts of another yellow flower.

"Next girl! What is your full name? Have you got a middle name?"

20

"Yes, miss. My name is Mary Daffodil Davies."

Gasps and sniggers preceded cries of: "No it's not, miss! She's not called Daffodil! She's Mary Davies from up Philly's!"

After a kindly but not over-brief lecture to the class on telling tales, I was registered as plain Mary Davies, much to my chagrin and shame at being caught out. How was I to know that not all flowers could be used for people's names? And what unappreciated patriotic tendencies I showed in choosing a daffodil!

Being the front room of a miner's terraced cottage, the shop was essentially small. This however had its advantages in that you hardly needed to move from the centre spot to reach whatever was required. Also it always looked overcrowded and, after a delivery of various commodities, desperately overcrowded, but this gave it a homely, friendly air, rather like a wholesome Aladdin's Cave. On the wall adjacent to our living room were several shelves stacked with jars of sweets: Mintoes, jelly-babies, nut clusters, Welsh mints, humbugs, chocolate eclairs, peardrops, treacle toffees, lemon bonbons, Pontefract cakes and aniseed balls to name but some.

Lest all this rich fare should make you ill, a lower shelf held boxes of aspirin and Phensic, tins of liver salts, Rennies, Beecham's powders and pills, Laxipurg, vaseline and cough medicines.

Various bars of chocolate, Milky Lunch, toffee, nougat, coconut ice and other wrapped chocolates such as raspberry ruffles, Jamieson's chocolate assortment, Quality Street and Roses were laid out for careful display in the window, together with the newest line in confectionery brought by the supplier on every visit.

Cheaper sweets for young children — lollipops, candy-sticks, barley-sugar twists, licorice shapes, Cherry Lips, a bottle containing little twigs of chewy Spanish root and the inevitable jar of sherbet — were placed prominently on a higher shelf behind the window, where youngsters could get their eager, out-stretched hands on them with the minimum of delay. All they had to do was point and pay. One question my father least liked to hear was: "What have you got for tuppence, Mr Davies?" His invariable answer, after a deep sigh and a *sotto voce* "Jesus", was: "If you got two hours to spare, love, I'll tell you." Few if any children understood or even suspected his irony.

The worst question though went like this: "Have you got any birthday cards that will do for my mother's brother-in-law, Mr

Davies?" His eyes would glaze over; he would smile and say, "Oh, excuse me a moment, will you?" and fetch my more patient mother, or failing her my reluctant self, to serve the irresolute card-customer. Card-customers lingered, fingering through what seemed hundreds of cards before deciding on the first they'd looked at, and in the process disarranging the lot so that 'Aged 4' was mixed up with 'Happy Birthday, Daughter' and sympathy cards were interleaved with 'Congratulations on Passing Your Exam!'. My mother was quite happy to serve, chatting away about the weather, the washing, the buses, Porth, Ponty, the market, the mountain... No matter if the customer didn't reply, she would prattle on; it was rather like Music While You Work. While I, when called upon to serve a card-customer, could always read a book for half an hour. Meanwhile my father would have a well-deserved sit down, a cup of tea and a smoke, gathering together the reserves of energy necessary to return to the shop and tackle the disarray left in the card-boxes. Had he had to witness the process of choosing and discarding that created the mess, there would undoubtedly have been occasional cases of strangled customers on the Tump.

People, women especially, liked my mother to serve them as she was always ready for a chat and generous to a fault. If someone required cotton of a colour not available in the shop cotton-box, she would march to the kitchen, rummage about in a dresser drawer until she found an approximation of what was needed, unwind a few yards which she would bite off with her teeth and take to the customer. If the cotton was needed for a sewing machine, she would give them the whole reel, telling them to bring back what was left, if any, when they had finished with it. Frequently people would come too late to buy bread and, looking round the breadless shop:

"Oh, you 'aven' got no bread left, 'ave you, Mrs Davies?"

"No, gul, sorry. All gone. If you'd said earlier, I'd have kept you a loaf."

"Oh, duw, I thought I had enough for Griff's sandwiches for 'is lunchbox tomorrow, but I 'aven't."

"Wait a minute. I'll go and see how much we've got."

Mam would disappear to the back kitchen, get the bread bin out of the dresser cupboard, chop our loaf in halves and return with one half for the customer. "There you are! I can spare you this. Will that do?"

"Oh, thank you, Mrs Davies. That'll do lovely. How much do I owe you now then, for this?"

"Oh, that's orright, Mrs Bassett. It's on'y a bit off ours."

Occasionally a bit later on I would hear: "Mary, run down Hafod and get me a small loaf, will you? There's a good girl!"

In my early years I can remember sacks of sugar, soda, flour and bone meal standing on the shop floor and irregularly hewn chunks of butter, lard and cheese on grey marble slabs, black-handled knives thrust into them with long, honed and hollow blades.

My mother was a farmer's daughter, one of ten children, and in the early twentieth century living on a farm meant living in comparative isolation. As a result, until she was ten she spoke the language of the country, not the town — Welsh. Throughout her life she never forgot the Welsh language and various Welsh-speaking inhabitants of Trehafod came to the shop ostensibly to buy but in reality to speak in Welsh with my mother.

One such was a middle-aged lady from the Top Street known locally as Old Mrs Knifey. I believe her official name was Mrs Williams and she was a north Welsh woman. She was tall, thin as a blade and gaunt, sallow-complexioned with amazingly hollowed black eyes. Everything about her apart from her face was black: dress, stockings, shoes and hair (middle-parted, wispy and in a bun). She always bought loose soda and Marie biscuits and was the nearest living thing I'd ever seen to the picture of a black-hatted harridan astride a broomstick in my story book. What is more, my language seemed as foreign to her as Welsh was to me. I was quite sure she was a witch. Normally quite a chatty child, I would hide behind my mother, clutching firmly at the skirt of her pinny, and, peering round her hips, shuffle forwards or sideways as she moved to get the biscuits or weigh out the soda. Sometimes I was outrageously tactless and insensitive in the woman's presence.

"Mam, has she got a black cat in her house?"

Then, quieter:

"I think she's a witch."

An unoccupied hand would deliver a quick flail backwards, warning me to shut up. Once she had gone I was more voluble in my questions about her suspected sorcery, but my mother would lose patience with me.

"Old Mrs Knifey is a very nice, Welsh lady, the old-fashioned sort. She's very lonely since her husband died. Now don't be so *twp*. Witch, indeed. There's no such thing as witches on broomsticks," she would say pragmatically, attempting for once to destroy foolish childish illusions.

As I grew up I served old Mrs Knifey in the shop many times, but always denoted a smidgeon of disappointment flashing across her face when I, rather than my Welsh-speaking mother, would arrive to attend to her purchases. Her appearance belied her disposition, as, though shy, she was intelligent, kindly and concerned, and if she spoke English a little idiosyncratically it was with an enchanting Welshness not evident in other Trehafod people.

The only other time she was seen was on Sunday morning and evening, sombrely dressed, lankily and hurriedly sweeping down Church Hill, the slope adjacent to St Barnabas', negotiating the rough terrain of the short cut with nimble adroitness, clutching her Welsh prayer-book on her way to Bethel Chapel in lower Trehafod. We assumed she lived on Marie biscuits as she was never seen out going shopping, and as for the soda — her house must have been a paradise of purity — as was probably her soul.

Years later, when I was a student at the University College of Aberystwyth, she made a brief incursion into my life again.

I was awestruck by the greatness of some of the teachers I came across there: Professor Gwyn Jones of the English Department, whose work on the *Mabinogion* and the Icelandic Sagas was internationally acclaimed; Mr Earnshaw of the same department; Professor Treharne and Richard Cobb, History; Jac L. Jones, the Welsh professor; the clever and handsome Edward Nevin, of the Economics Department; and in Geography, Harold Carter and Professor E.G. Bowen, whose book, *Wales*, had at school been our A level Geography bible.

One of the early letters from home informed me that old Mrs Knifey was glad I'd gone to Aber because one of her brothers was there. Later my mother wrote, "Old Mrs Knifey's brother is a professor of geography". Mam didn't know much about professors, lecturers, readers, researchers and the like, so I more or less ignored this item of news, until a subsequent letter made me blink in amused disbelief: "His name is Professor Bowen". "No, can't be," I wrote back. "You must be mistaken." Never could I imagine old Mrs

Knifey from Top Street having anything to do with the great Professor Bowen, esteemed author of geographical tomes and the *only* professor of geography in Wales at that time.

Towards the end of the year, Professor Bowen announced to the vast and adulatory first year geography class that he had to go to South Wales and therefore our next week's lecture would be cancelled. The following letter from home was both sad and triumphant. Old Mrs Knifey had died and, yes, Professor Bowen was her brother, because he had come for the funeral and had been in the shop, OUR SHOP!, and Mam had told him I was at Aber, and yes, he knew, as his sister had told him, but he didn't know me, and he wanted to thank Mam for her kindness to his sister over the years. I was flabbergasted.

A glance at the South Wales telephone directory will reveal a proliferation of surnames such as: Lewis, Jones, Davies, Williams, Watkins, Evans, Thomas, Smith, Rees, Harris, Jenkins, Pugh, Morris and Morgan, and so of course it was in Trehafod. Although as far as I could see we were a flourishing and healthy community, there was a lot of inter-marriage as people loved the Tump, didn't go very far away from it and married the girl or boy next door. There were never any empty houses. The only ones that became available were after a death, and those would be snapped up practically before the body was cold. You could bet that if there were a family of Robertses living in Bottom Street and another in Second Street they were cousins. As a result practically all the names were familiarly Welsh and although there was never a very great variety of name, no one ever mixed the people up.

On fine days, and it was usually fine in my childhood, ladies, sometimes clad purposefully in turbans and always in pinafores, usually wielding a sweeping brush or putting out a bucket of ashes for the ash-cart, would espy another lady similarly employed, and soon, having abandoned their chores to lean on their brooms or against the lintel, would have a well-deserved doorstep chat and watch the world go by.

"Young Mrs Lewis — you know, Mrs Jenkins's oldest daughter, Second Street — is expecting."

"No, already? Only been married 'bout three weeks, 'aven't she?"

"Aye, and Maggie May told me that her friend — you know, Jane Jones, Pleasant View — she's expecting as well. But don't say, will you?"

"Ne-ever! Duw, duw, she's not even married yet. 'Aven't been engaged long."

"No, I know. I must say she's been looking a bit peaky lately. Never mind, their kids will be company for each other."

The women would have a little giggle, then move to another topic of Tump-shattering importance.

There were names originating from other parts of these isles, such as McTiffin, which I always thought had something to do with chocolate, Daley and O'Rourke, and even some foreigners. But their names were too long and vowel-less for Tump tongues, so they were simply 'the Poles' or 'the Czechs' — except for the Polish youngster called Dragon, whose name everybody remembered — and one diffident old man known as 'Russian'. How he had found his way to the Tump, goodness knows. A man of few words, he was employed in the Pontypridd chain works.

"How are you today, Russian?" my mother would ask.

"Oll right, Meesis Daviss. Some Woodbines, pleasse."

And, purchase completed, off he would shuffle, beaming and nodding.

The other type of name abounding would be homely ones such as Hawkins, Hurley, Hole and Hemmings, made homelier by completely ignoring the aspirates. Then there were the families of Button (including one, Pearl), Whatley, Luckwell (whose name singularly belied their fortunes), Emery, Eynon, Cook, Curtis, Jinks, Bevan and Minto, all good, straightforward names with no pretensions, like the inhabitants. No two ways about pronouncing them, although some young residents were particular about the pronunciation of their surnames.

One day a small person with an elfin face and tiny, fair, wispy plaits tied with bright ribbons and sticking out almost at right angles to her ears, came into the shop. I had never seen her before.

"Oh, 'ullo. What's your name, then?"

"Tracey." (With a flat 'a'.)

"Oh, Tracey Jones, is it?" I picked "Jones" (pronounced the usual way) as it was possibly the most common surname around.

"No," she said, philosophically and absent-mindedly, big eyes moving round looking at the sherbet lollies, dolly mixtures and bubble gum,

"Tracey Jones" (pronounced Jonss).

If Mr Botham came to Trehafod, he would probably be Mr Bottom, but a local Mrs McLoughlin-Watkins was known as Mrs Whatsername.

I remember some people moving into lower Trehafod and coming to services at St Barnabas' Church opposite the shop. "What are they called then?" someone asked my mother.

"Faulkner."

"Faulkner?! My goodness, there's posh!"

One village lady called Cissie had unfortunately buried her Englishman husband surnamed Sparrowhawk. She was left with two children, Gloria and Lennie, and later made a long, happy marriage with Olly Pugh, pigeon-fancier and discoverer of the body in the pond. Gloria became Miss Pugh, but Lennie retained his father's name and went away to live with his grandmother in Mitcham, Surrey. He later moved to South Africa, where he became a well-known actor and married the great grand-daughter of General Smuts. Before his departure he came into the shop and my mother served him. Having a great interest in everybody, she asked him how he was, what he was, where he was and so on, but afterwards came back into the house a little perplexed.

"What on earth is that man's name?" she asked. "I had a long chat with him. He's a lovely boy, but now he's grown up and moved away, I couldn't hardly call him Lennie, could I?"

No one knew why not, exactly. "Sparrowhawk," I said.

My mother put her hand in horror to her lips. Eyes and mouth opened wide. "Oh, no. *Mawrth*! I knew it was something to do with birds." She bit her bottom lip in dismay. "I called him Mr Scarecrow!"

Once a week there was great agitation in the shop for the Corona pop delivery from Thomas and Evans Ltd from their factory in Porth. As many pairs of hands as could be found to help, often and usually customers, pitched in willingly to remove empty bottles from the floor at the back of the shop onto the counter where the pop men would clatter them into wooden crates and, two in each hand, sixteen empties in all, rush out and hurl them noisily, force-fully but accurately onto the orange wooden shelves on the sides of the pop lorry. Collisions were many, both inside and outside the shop, but despite the lack of space inside it was far safer than outside in the path of the scurrying, crate-carrying pop men. Unfortunate customers who happened to be on the buying side of the counter cowered in the corner against the door leading into the house, while those on the selling side wisely stayed where they were. Crates of bottles of Dandelion and Burdock, Apple Crush, Ginger Beer, Cream Soda and the usual lemonades, limeades, orangeades and cherryades were brought in and lined up on the counter for trans-portation to the shelves by the bruised helpers. Invariably one of the bottles with its fingernail-breaking spring top and orange rubber flange would be opened and the contents unceremoniously con-sumed as the bottle was passed around, for this was thirsty work. If a shaft of sunlight filtered through to the back wall, the pop was transformed into clear, sparkling, iridescent greens, yellows and auburns, bathing the whole shop in a warm reflected glow. At such times, surrounded by friendly, smiling people, the joking pop men, the shop tidy with all the bottles of pop neatly stacked and the tea-party to come, life was good.

We had lots of tea-parties when I was young. Whenever a traveller came to deliver or collect an order, the business concluded, he would take a cup of tea with my mother and me in the back kitchen. Naturally each week all the pop workers and any customer who had suffered the trauma of the delivery and had been brave enough to stay came to the tea party too. A jug of milk, a bowl of sugar and a plate piled high with Welsh cakes still warm from the bakestone were laid out and everyone helped themselves as my mother poured out the almost black tea.

"Come on, Mr Dando and Ronnie," (the pop men, the senior of whom was always addressed formally) "help yourselves, come on now."

Holding up his Welsh cake as evidence, Mr Dando would say: "We're all right, thank you, Mrs Davies. Mustn't eat too much between meals. I got to watch out for my stomach, see. Lovely Welsh cakes these are, too. Like 'em a bit brown, I do. Can't a-bear those old pale 'uns."

"Got many more calls today, Mr Dando? Come on, Mrs Thomas, gul, have another Welsh cake. Another cup of tea Mr Morris?"

"Yes, up Abercynon after this, Mrs Davies, then back to the depot, two more deliveries round Porth, then 'ome."

"Oh, not too bad then, Mr Dando. Sugar, Mr Evans? Oh, never mind the crumbs, Lizzie-Ann, I'll sweep them up after, in a winkie. How's your mother today, Mrs Rees? Still under the doctor?"

And so it went on for an action-packed quarter of an hour of lovely, inconsequential cross-chat. These impromptu tea-parties delighted me far more than any formal birthday tea-party with pretty dresses, presents, jelly and blancmange, chunks and cake. In fact, when I was allowed a postwar birthday party, my list of guests included the pop men, Mrs Thomas, Mrs Rees, Lizzie-Ann, Mr Evans, Mr Morris, Olly Pugh and no children at all.

Pop days were undoubtedly the highlight of the week. I loved the pretty colours of the full shelves of bottles, and when my mother was cooking dinner, and I had to run and serve, I was most reluctant to part with a bottle of pop. My heart would sink to hear: "Four bottles of pop, two red, one orange, and one ice-cream soda, please".

"Aven't got any red, sorry."

"Oh, yes, you 'ave, I can see some there, look, on the bottom shelf behind the ginger beer."

"Oh, aye, so we have."

And, handing the customer the bottles, I could hardly restrain a baleful pout, and to spite her would give all the change in ha'pennies.

As the week wore on and the pop gradually sold, but with a spurt on Sundays, the shelves looked sad and bare and the wall-paper of the former front room was revealed in all its antique, flowery yellowness. However, there was always another visit from the pop men to look forward to before long.

One of the great characters known and seen round the area was Paddy Collins, who sold us vinegar. He lived in Danylan — a few streets also perched on the hillside just north of Pontypridd. Some people called him "the Cockle-man", for he also traded in these little sandy delicacies, most "Paddy", and my mother, "Mr Collins". As his name suggested, he was not Welsh, and despite having

29

lived in Danylan for most of his life maintained a strong, delightful southern Irish accent. He was a very successful tradesman, known to everyone and doubtless part of his charm was his accent and language peppered with holy exclamations. Also, he could not speak, only shout. Not for him whispered negotiations. Everybody knew his business and even when he came into the house for his cup of tea after delivering the vinegar, people out in the street could hear exactly what was going on.

My mother adored him and he would get a piece of apple tart as well as a Welsh cake. He knew and shouted to practically everyone, no matter whether he was on the main road, perilously perched on the side of his cart, holding the reins of his lively nag as it pranced smartly along, or generously weighing out cockles in the street from a metal scoop into enamel bowls. On my way home from school I might hear: "Mary Davies, me little darlin', how are ye this lovely day? And how's yer good mother then, Lord bless her soul?" He never got a reply, because by the end of the sentence he would be fifty yards further on, yelling at someone else, waving his arms in greeting as the cockles and empty vinegar barrels bounced about behind him on his cart. Fortunately his trusty pony knew the way and transported him safely along the roads.

His most distinguishing feature was his black eye-patch, but despite this he didn't miss a thing and there was enough sparkle in his other eye for both anyway. He was a strong, vigorous and gallant man even into old age.

"Oh, Mr Collins, you could charm the spots off a leopard," my mother would say.

"Ah, Mrs Davies, when 'tis such charming people as yourself and darlin' young Mary Davies here, 'tis no difficult task, 'pon the Word of the good Lord," and he would wink at me several times with his good eye.

He had a son, Michael, a good-looking man also with laughing eyes, who increasingly accompanied his father as the years went by, holding the reins, sitting on the other side of the cart, balancing it. He was slightly less extrovert in manner, and gave the travelling out-fit a safer, roadworthier appearance. People were glad to see him and there were fewer anxious looks when he was in charge. Paddy could now shout to the passers-by and wave his arms without the hindrance of driving. The pony also looked happier and high-stepped along without blinkers when Michael was there. The son was still unmarried when middle-aged and this appeared to bother his father.

"Oh, Mary Davies," he would say to me, then aged nine or ten, "young Michael Collins here is waiting for you to be his bride. Holy Virgin, you'd make him a good wife, if you grow up anything like your own dear mother, to be sure, Lord bless us."

Hearing this more than once caused me some anxiety as I had not the slightest intention of being anyone's bride or wife. All I wanted was for my life to stay as it was for ever.

"Oh, they're very wealthy, you know, and Michael's the only son, so some girl will be lucky some day."

What wealth had to do with anything puzzled me. I didn't understand my mother sometimes. You didn't need to be wealthy to roam around the mountain and play in the village streets.

Once the wooden cask of vinegar with the metal bands around it had been manoeuvred into the shop it had to be tapped. This was done by my father when he came home from work at the BOAC test-beds. With a wooden mallet he would knock a little wooden plug into the barrel, push the tap in firmly, then heave the cask upright onto a pedestal, placing the drip-bowl underneath. People liked Mr Collins's vinegar as it was not watered down, and as it was loose all sorts of receptacles were brought to carry it in: bottles, bowls, jars, jugs — and one chamber-pot. I didn't mind serving vinegar, and developed a good aim, nonchalantly displayed, when pouring it.

Certain times of the year assured excellent sales of some commodities, though we were never without them at other periods. These were candles and block salt. If the gas supply was low, or in later years when there was a power cut and electricity didn't enlighten people's lives, customers would stream into the shop, itself lit by candles and a paraffin lamp. My father didn't need to ask the ghostly, shadowy people what they wanted, just how many, though there was the occasional misunderstanding.

"A dozen, Mrs Roberts?"

"Oh, no, Mr Davies. Dick isn't so bad as that. I only want one tin of Laxipurg, thanks. That'll do until tomorrow."

And both would chuckle, but my father would apologise gracious-
ly, as the customer was always right. "Oh, I do beg your pardon, Mrs
Roberts. My mistake." And after a few seconds' searching in a
drawer in the flickering light, out would come an elastic-beribboned
card.

"There you are, Mrs Roberts. One tin of Laxipurg. Fourpence,
please."

Meanwhile my mother and I would be dodging around each
other, fetching and serving hundreds of candles for the flow of
grateful people eager to return home as the saviour with light.
Philosophy at such moments was rife.

"Well, I dunno. Good job we got the old candle. You can rely on
that, but not on all these modern, new-fangled inventions. Hmmm!
So much for 'letric. Not very reliable, is it?"

During snowy, frosty and icy weather there would be a rush on
salt and extra supplies were brought in of best blocks from North-
wich in Cheshire. Though the blocks were wrapped and solid, grains
of salt would drop through the paper; after a few dozen had been
transported to the counter, the shop floor would soon be as salted
as the icy pavement outside. However, the reverse principle applied,
and we would be slipping and sliding around, losing our footing on
the inside surface while those outside were afforded a sure, firm
walkway. Customers looked in amazement at the slithering Davieses and must have thought we were putting on a winter ice-spec-
tacular for their delectation. Fortunately damage was limited to a
few sore bottoms.

In the candle and salt seasons we saw people who never came to
the shop at other times, perhaps people who hadn't paid a bill in
the past or who had had an altercation with my mother, disagreeing
with her politics, and most did in the Rhondda. My father was
always the soul of old-world courtesy and discretion in the shop. It
was not for nothing he had in his book-case *Manners Maketh Man*
and *Etiquette for All Occasions*. At such times all customers, no
matter how faithful, were, naturally, served with the required product and with a smile. My father, using a basic economic concept,
might have raised the price by a ha'penny per candle or a penny per
block of salt since the previous week, but this was mitigated by the
fact that he would put a limit on the number to be sold per person,
so that it was fairly allocated.

"Six blocks of salt, please, Mr Davies."

"Sorry, only two per person, Mrs Morris — one to go under each arm, see, love."

"Oh, orright then. Only I wanted some for Mrs 'Unkins next door an' all. Never mind, she can have a bit of mine. How much is that, Mr Davies?"

"That will be a tanner altogether, Mrs Morris."

"Oh, gone up, 'ave it?"

"Yes, Mrs Morris. Went up last delivery, last Friday."

By the time the icy weather had finished, block salt from Cheshire via Philly's must have covered the majority of pavements in Trehafod and certainly all those on the Tump, not to mention the garden steps and paths leading to the lavatories, as well as the daily diet of boiled potatoes.

One part of the shop, the narrow, deep shelves above the till and below the bottles of sweets, was particularly my father's domain. It contained a fascinating array of bottles, boxes, tins and packets of varying smallish shapes and sizes, and was known to my mother and me as the Pharmacy. Here my father reigned supreme. People sought his advice which undoubtedly comforted and cured a large proportion of the Tump population of various minor complaints and illnesses. Men, but mainly women, even came up from lower Trehafod to tell him of their ailments and see what wonders Jack's medicaments could perform. On such occasions, the shop was not Philly's or Corner Shop but Jack's, as my father was the consultant.

During the day my father was at work in the BOAC plant in Caerphilly, so his 'patients' would come to the 'surgery' in the evening when they knew he was home. At the weekend if someone came in looking pale, sick or staggering, and I happened to be in attendance, I would say, "Hang on," — and in some cases they literally had to — "I'll get my father."

My mother had a more mature, sympathetic approach. "Oh, dear, not feeling too well, are you, Mrs Wilcox?" Often the reply was a weak, "No, I'm feeling awful bad today."

"Wait a minute, and I'll fetch Jack. Look, lean against the counter by there. Or shall I fetch you a chair?" — which she often did. The very poorly ones were offered a cup of tea.

Fortunately my father knew most of his clients' habits.

"Oh, not looking too well today, Mrs Pring. Had a good night last night, did you? Never mind, a tin of Andrews' Health Salts will sort you out."

And sure enough Mrs Pring would later be seen, fit and well, descending Bryn Eirw Hill for another good night out at the Vaughan's Arms.

"Oh, Mr Davies, Danny come home with a bad back today. It hurts him when he breathes deep, like."

"Oh, yes, Mr Davies, Danny wouldn't miss his football. Filthy dirty he was after it, too. Pouring with rain it was last Saturday."

"Probably pulled a back muscle, Mrs Jones. Here you are, try some of this Elliman's Rub. You got to rub it in good and hard just where the pain is."

And so it went on, my father dispensing wisdom and sympathy along with his Little Liver Pills, Seidlitz, Soothing and Beecham's Powders, Friar's Balsam, Germolene, Zambuck, Corn Plasters, Pads ands Paste, Vick's Vapour Rub and Eucalyptus Oil, a few drops of which children loved to put on their handkerchieves whether they had a cold or not. From November to February the prevalent aroma of Hafod School was not of books, chalk and ink but of eucalyptus from Jack's.

Mostly my father would leave the wholesale buying to my mother, who largely took the advice of travellers over a cup of tea and a biscuit in the kitchen, but when it was time to order for the Pharmacy he was strictly in charge and she had a list for the man from Stothert's of Atherton or Sleath's of Merthyr Tydfil.

These names were prominent in my childhood and I had enormous respect for their powers. Sleath's produced among other things Laxipurg, a popular line, and one of Stothert's major sellers was Dr Maclean's Stomach Powders. Perhaps the most surprising pharmaceutical product was 'Elasto Tablets for the Relief of Aching Legs', which I assumed had been purposely manufactured for us, perched as we were at the top of two hills. I once asked my father if he gave one of these free to the ladies who toiled up from lower Trehafod to see him, as he donated a jelly baby to the wide-eyed youngsters deliberating over their penny purchases.

People were of the universal opinion that if they felt unwell it wasn't worth the bother of catching the bus to Porth to see the doctor until they'd first been to Jack's, because more often than not he'd cure them.

"What you doing with a shop, Mr Davies?" was frequently a question asked of him. "You should have been a doctor, mun." And no doubt had he been given the chance he would have made the grade. However, his medical knowledge was respected by all, for had he not passed the First Aid section of his Mining Safety Officer's exams with flying colours?

Sometimes the client was clearly incurable with my father's modest assortment of pills and potions. At such times he would take down a tome entitled *The Universal Home Doctor and Medical Adviser (Illustrated)*, listen to the location and type of pain, ache or discomfort, rummage through the book for a few seconds, read for a few minutes, then pronounce: "If I were you, I'd go and see Dr Clarke, Mrs Bradfield. I don't think it's anything serious, mind, but it's best to be on the safe side." He would never tell them what he thought was wrong, but would none the less mention it to my mother, the soul of discretion in such matters, and nine times out of ten he was right.

"Harry Griffiths is having trouble with his bowels. Doesn't know what he's doing, poor chap. Got a bad pain going right round to the back. Sounds like liver trouble to me."

When he thought the customer was really ill, he would offer to telephone the doctor for them from the kiosk on Sant's Hill, opposite Bevan's greengrocery shop. People were eternally grateful for this, as at that time telephones were new-fangled inventions that did strange things and made strange noises and which local inhabitants didn't like at all. Secondly, this meant saving the bother of a bus journey and fare, and my father invariably in his generosity would stand the cost of the phone call. I loved to accompany him on these occasions and would squeeze into the box beside him as he manipulated the coins, the various noises, the dialling and the receiver. In high seriousness and standing on ceremony he would say, clearly enunciating each syllable as though broadcasting to the other side of the earth:

"This is John Davies, speaking from Trehafod. I have a message for Dr Clarke of Porth. He is required to attend with some urgency Mr Harold Griffiths, Woodfield Terrace, Trehafod. I repeat, Mr Harold Griffiths, of Woodfield Terrace, Trehafod. Thank you."

35

He wouldn't wait for any reply or indulge in conversation, but would put down the phone, message given, job done, and that was that. His telephone style never changed, and was the same even twenty years later, to the surprise and consequent respectful amusement of his son-in-law and grandchildren. In a strange way he pre-dated his time in this; his phone manner would have been perfect for the telephone answering machine.

Then we would go back to the shop, take over from my mother and, the drama forgotten for the time being, would get on with the really serious business of serving the dolly mixtures.

Vinegar, candles, rock salt and medicaments were all very well, but as far as I was concerned the shop's main reason for existence was to stock sweets and chocolates. I didn't bother too much about the trade part of shop-keeping as long as it was well stocked. During the war there was of course a singular lack of sweet confectionery to be had and the little shop looked sad, grey, miserable and bare for a lot of the time. Imagine the excitement, not only of my family but of the entire neighbourhood, when the navy-blue van of Mr Bale, the sweet wholesaler, arrived once every blue moon from Merthyr. Word soon spread around the Tump, and shortly to the rest of Trehafod, it seemed, and before the boxes could be unloaded from the van there would be a queue of war-deprived people, hungry for sweets, lining up along Bryn Eirw Street, stopping the residents from getting to their front doors. On one of these occasions, Billy Watkins, No 34, who had been enjoying a nap, was woken up and went out in the street thinking the war was over to see all the excited people milling around. He must have been sorely disappointed to be told: "Oh, no, it's just Philly's — they're having some sweets delivered."

Apart from the fact that he was the purveyor of goodies, so the God of Sweets in my eyes, I liked Mr Bale best of all the salesmen who came to the house. He was a large man with a round, kindly, bespectacled face, with eyes that were smiling even when his mouth was not. But what struck me most was the gentle way in which he spoke, with a cultured accent and in the politest manner. He would show my mother, or father if he happened to be home from work, the list of his stock, and after everything ordered he would say: "Thank you. And the next?"

"I'll have a box of three dozen Rolos, Mr Bale."

"Thank you. And the next?"

"Now let me see. Oh, five dozen lollipops, please."

"Thank you. And the next?"

It amazed me that he should be the one to say thank you to us, as at his war-time appearance I felt we should be going down on our knees before him and saying something like: "Oh good, delightful Mr Bale, God of Sweets and Chocolates, most excellent strong man, thank you a thousand times for bringing your blue van to us with its assorted confectionery. We promise to sell them to people who will appreciate them and not gobble them up too fast. Likewise me." Incomprehensibly, my parents didn't care too much for sweets.

To me Mr Bale was the epitome of good breeding and my admiration for Merthyr was total. What with Sleath's pharmaceutical products and Mr Bale, it must be a very fine and posh place indeed. What is more, he didn't want me to be anyone's bride or wife, although the thought did cross my mind that in the unlikely event of my ever getting married it would be to someone like Mr Bale, especially if he was in the same line of work.

If Mr Bale's blue moon visit was in the winter, there was less likelihood of a queue forming outside as it was too dark to see the navy-blue van, which had no markings on it in war-time (possibly Mr Bale was in fear of being mobbed if he advertised the fact that his van contained sweets), and people would be discouraged from outside queuing by the exposed corner position atop Bryn Eirw and Church Hills and the easterly wind sweeping down the street.

Then my mother would send me, well wrapped up with a muffler, to certain houses to tell the most loyal customers that we had had a sweet delivery. Clutching their ration books, they would congregate in the dim, gaslit shop with the blackout blind, each one on arrival discreetly knocking at the door which was quickly opened and shut, so that the place seemed to be hosting a secret society meeting, with everyone speaking in hushed tones. Money was no problem for sweet purchases in those days, but customers were confined by their limited allocation of sweet coupons.

These were a real nuisance and had to be cut out of the ration books, sometimes tiny little quarter-inch bits of paper which stuck to my father's fingers and drove him mad, or fell through cracks in the floor. All had to be accounted for and the difficulty was compounded by each month having different letters and black and white letters having different values.

"Jesus, you've got to have the patience of Job to do this job," I often heard my father say. Indeed it did make the task of sweet selling very slow and trying, so perhaps it was just as well we didn't see Mr Bale all that often.

There were two other shops close by, Terry Stores and Cobner's, but never was there any question of rivalry between us. In fact we were more of a cooperative of shop-keepers, and Mr Ossie James, who came down on the Cardiff bus from Pentre every day to manage Terry's, often stopped on his way to and from work to have a mutually sympathising chat with my mother about constantly changing prices, this down a ha'penny, that up tuppence, unreliable suppliers and hard-to-please customers, among other things. Often, if Mr James ran out of a product, he would send his assistant down the street to us.

"We're out of Craven A, Mrs Davies. Could you let us have twenty packets of ten, please. We'll let you have them back tomorrow, O.K?"

It always was okay, and we lived a hundred yards apart in harmony. If we were short of something urgently required, I, when not at school, was the messenger for Philly's. My father particularly hated not being able to provide a customer with what he wanted. He would never say, as I have often heard said since those days, "Sorry, love, there's no demand for it". If someone is asking for something there is clearly a demand for it. Even if it meant catching the bus to Porth or Ponty to buy the required object, he would get whatever it was if he thought the shop could or should have been stocking it, and would say to the disappointed client, "I'll have some for you tomorrow, Bert, on the dot."

Sometimes I was sent on erroneous and futile errands to Terry's. A lady might come in and knock impatiently on the counter, shouting urgently to attract attention. My mother would run from the back kitchen, for the shop was not constantly attended. There she would encounter the excited face of a customer-neighbour longing to impart some news she had been sworn to secrecy not to tell.

38

Conversely, quieter, weepier and far less commanding tones of "Shop" might bring her face to face with a lady whose heart, bursting with sad news, needed comfort and consolation from a sympathetic listener.

Whatever the case, the confider would be brought into the back kitchen and, a cup of tea under way:

"Mary, run up to Terry's and get me a tin of condensed milk, there's a good girl."

"But Mam, we've got some in the shop."

"No, we haven't."

"Yes, we 'ave. Next to the peaches. I'll fetch a tin for you."

"Er... Well, I don't like that make. Go and buy a different one."

Before I could ask what on earth she wanted a tin of condensed milk for, as we never used it, I was given some money, ushered out and, with me safely out of earshot, Mam and the visitor would discuss the problem or the news.

It was always to Terry's Stores I was sent, as they would guarantee a good twenty minutes' wait, and as Ossie was always short-staffed I usually ended up helping to put up orders and sometimes deliver them if the box was not too heavy or the distance too far. So my mother and friend could often chat undisturbed for a good hour.

I quite liked going to Terry's Stores. It had sawdust over the floor and if you had a really long, tedious wait you could draw pictures in it with your foot. I sometimes got so absorbed in my art work, I lost my turn to be served.

There was a small room off to the side where the vegetables, but mainly sacks of potatoes, were kept. Various neighbourhood boys who worked for a bar or two of chocolate, frequently mitching from school, served these, often bowling or booting them into the scales, as Ossie and the assistant wore white coats and were only allocated two each per week. Terry Stores precariously overhung a dried-up valley, or possibly a former incline, and from a small window at the end of the shop there was a good view of the main road, the lower end of the colliery and over to Llwyncelyn. So what with the sawdust, the view and the antics of the mitchers, it was never a boring place to be.

Occasionally on arrival back home I discovered I had completely misread the situation and my mother, the visitor departed, really did want a certain purchase.

"Oh, at last! Come on, gul. Where've you been? I was about to send out a search party. You've been gone an hour and I want the gravy browning to make your father's dinner. He'll be here soon."

"Shop! Shop!"

"Oh, hell's bells, go and see who that is, Mari fach, there's a good girl."

Cobner's sweet and cigarette shop was a dear little place almost opposite the main colliery entrance and even smaller than ours — much smaller, in fact. It looked as though it had been converted from the passageway or downstairs corridor of a house, for there was only just enough room for Mr Cobner to squeeze in behind the narrow counter above the grey flagstoned floor. No more than three people could stand in the shop, and they were required to stand side by side. There were often more customers waiting their turn outside to come in than there were inside waiting to be served. And if you happened to be the furthest third person from the door, the two next to you had to shuffle backwards or sideways out of the shop in order to let you leave. Mr Cobner had no fat people as customers for the wooden slatted green door was scarcely more than two feet wide and as the door opened inwards, thus further restricting the space, they would get stuck. The sweets were in jars in recesses on the wall behind the counter or in boxes in the window, and the cigarettes and tobacco were on shelves under the counter. Miners buying Woodbines on their way to and from the colliery waited while Mr Cobner, turning sideways, bent down and scrabbled about in the region of his knees. I often thought how much more convenient it would have been if Mr Cobner had been a smaller man, as he was broad of frame and at least six feet tall. But his movements were very adroit and he knew exactly where he could turn or bend without knocking things over or hurting his person or getting wedged. Mrs Cobner was a small, neat person and negotiating the little shop was altogether easier for her.

There was one thing I envied them, and that was their door-bell. The door opened, a little bell would sweetly tinkle away up above, and Mr or Mrs Cobner would appear from their house to the side of the shop through a kind of conservatory at the rear, and nimbly dodge behind the counter, open at that end, and would be facing the customer in seconds. No need in Cobner's to stand stupidly

40

shouting "Shop! Shop!" to nobody in particular as was necessary in ours.

I wanted us to install a bell and nagged my ever-patient father every time I returned from an expedition to Cobner's shop.

"No, we don't want a bell, love, I've told you. Anyway, our door is always open, so how would it work? We can't leave a hand-bell on the counter, 'cos the rebels would pinch it, see?"

"Aw, come on, Dad."

"Anyway, I'd go scatty with a bell going tinkle-tinkle-tinkle all day long. You don't want me to go scatty, now, do you?"

So we never had a bell and people continued to shout "Shop!" and rap the counter. The only thing to be said for that method was that one could begin to recognise people's voices, and if for any reason you wished to avoid a certain person, you could persuade someone else to serve them.

"Aw, Mam. May Davies, Top Street, is in the shop. She saw me eating a sweet in church on Sunday night and she'll tell me off. Will you go, Mam?"

Or: "Oh, that Mrs Ball is in the shop. She's so *didoreth,* I'll be there all day. Be a good girl and go and serve her, Mari fach."

Strange though it may seem, living as I did in a sweet shop, I was a frequent customer of Mr Cobner's. He always had time for a bit of a chat and a joke, and there were three ways to run to his shop: down Bryn Eirw Hill and up the road, past the bus-stop; halfway down the hill and then across the rough ground behind the fish-shop and the undertaker's; or finally, following a narrow path across the side of a grassy slope adjoining Bryn Eirw, where you could build up running speed to take the steeper slope up to some allotments, then behind them and down the grassy bank to the main road. So there was variety in the expedition, as well.

One vivid memory remains in my mind: the war was just over, sweet coupons were no longer required, I had a threepenny bit in my pocket, and I was about to buy my first un-rationed sweets. I sat for some time on the grassy bank, watching the people going up and down the hill, a yellow and blue bus on its way to Ponty and boys playing on the football field by the river, then slowly, savouring the moment, made my way to Cobner's. I bought a packet of Rowntrees wine-gums, my first postwar sweets — and got some change.

41

CHAPTER FOUR

Jack

My father was born in Top Street, Trehafod, the third of four children (two girls and two boys), though the family originated from Machen via Caerphilly, and he was respected by all and sundry as a cultured man. Serious-minded and earnest, he had striven to improve himself and his position in the world despite leaving Hafod School at thirteen.

After working for his mother in the shop and bakehouse for a few years and seeing his mates more manfully employed down the mine, his thoughts wandered in that direction. His mother though, no doubt thinking the male version of the adage: 'Don't send your son down the mine, Mrs Worthington', tried to dissuade him. As often happens between parents and children, disapproval on one side leads to increased determination on the other, and he went to the Lewis Merthyr colliery as a carpenter's apprentice underground.

1914 took everyone by surprise, and ensuing recruitment drives fired my father with patriotic pride. He soon found himself in the uniform of the Welsh Guards in Caterham barracks, and didn't like it. He and some soul-mates took to drowning their misery in drink, far too much of it. That and a certain weakness in the lungs decided the Guards he was not for them and they released him. His discharge papers state he was unfit for military service because of tuberculosis, in those days normally a death sentence. Somehow or other he was cured of the disease and lived to the age of eighty-two, when his lungs finally succumbed to cancer. To his mother's delight, his tentative flirtation with the army was soon over.

Having thus far only toyed with his abilities, he determined the way forward was to pass exams, to have qualifications to his name, and enrolled at the Treforest School of Mines (now the Polytechnic of Wales) to follow a Safety Officer and Mines Inspector's sandwich course with the blessing of the Lewis Merthyr management who could see he was cut out for more mentally demanding work than making pit-props. He passed his exams with flying colours but frustration was to follow again when he was found physically lacking for the job with a serious eye complaint called nystagmus. So it was back to square one: his mother's shop. Still aiming at a profession more intellectually taxing than selling butter, he embarked on a correspondence course. A fine certificate from the International Correspondence Schools, London, hung above the piano in the middle room, proclaiming that John Davies was awarded the 'Diploma of the Complete Commercial Course this thirteenth Day of July, AD 1923, having been Examined and found Duly Qualified in the Subjects mentioned herein: Commercial Arithmetic; Handwriting; Single and Double Entry Book-keeping; Wholesale Merchants' and Foreign Merchants' Accounts; Manufacturers' and Cost Accounts; Companies Accounts; Business Systems; Spelling; Elements of English; Punctuation; Business Correspondence and Shorthand and Typewriting.' Well, armed with all this expertise, what young man wouldn't be ready to face the world?

That world was once more London, where he was offered a job with the Direct Trading Company. He stayed with them for some years and rose to the position of manager of one of their large grocery shops in Paddington, lodging in the house of a Welsh couple nearby. A growing disaffection with London and the Welshman's *hiraeth* for his native land eventually brought him back home.

The next job was selling books for the Waverley Book Company during the day and at night he followed another correspondence course, this time with the Bennett College, Sheffield, in history and commerce, as economics was sensibly called in those days. His employers, no doubt impressed by his diligence in self-improvement and his intelligence and courteous manner, made him an area manager, and he worked happily and lucratively in this field for many years. His enthusiasm for distance learning continued and, amazingly, he obtained a qualification in Jiu-Jitsu by correspondence, a Black Belt, no less!

Now reaching his mid-thirties, well set up with a motor car, a tall, slim, not unprepossessing-looking man of wiry strength, having thick if prematurely greying hair and weak sight in his pale blue eyes, with a fine nose rutted at the bridge by spectacles, it was well time he got himself wed — after all "it is a truth universally acknowledged that a single man in possession of a good fortune" (or not impecunious, in this case) "must be in want of a wife".

CHAPTER FIVE

Sal

My mother was the eighth child of William Richards, farmer, of Clawr y Plwyf, Mynyddislwyn, Monmouthshire and his wife, Mary, (née Davies, hence my name), who bore ten children in all, a perfectly balanced family of five boys and five girls.

My mother, Sarah, spoke little English for the first ten years of her life. Welsh dominated, and William was a great friend of the bard, Islwyn, at that time the Parch at the church of Mynyddislwyn, St Tudor's, almost atop the hill above the farm. My mother told me a memorable story about the building of the church early in the eighteenth century. Apparently the mortar for the stones wouldn't set, they couldn't get the walls straight on the rocky hill, parts of it kept falling down and altogether they had great trouble in erecting the building. The wind blew hard at those heights and one day a workman, taking a rest and listening to the wind, heard it say: "*Is-lwyn, Is-lwyn*" (lower down, lower down). At this point my mother would sound like the wind and move her hands with a windlike motion. Doubtless this was the voice of God. The workman transmitted his thoughts to his foreman and consequently they decided to abandon the original site and build the church under the brow of the hill. It went up like a bird with no problems in the construction and so bequeathed to man a fine view of Monmouthshire and Glamorgan from the top of the bell-tower. There is also a fine view of the church, majestically standing just below the hill-top, from the Sirhowy Valley below.

In 1902 the Richards family moved to Pontypridd. William had been offered the tenancy of a farm called Tydraw on the estate of Judge Gwilym Rhys-Williams of Miskin Manor. Compared with

Clawr y Plwyf, with its difficult terrain and limited agriculture on the steep slopes of Mynyddislwyn, Tydraw was like the Garden of Eden. The south-facing house, long, low and sturdy, nestles in under the protection of the gently sloping hill to the north which proceeds to assert itself into Gelliwion Mountain and the watershed before plunging down steeply into the valley of the Rhondda.

The fields were large and more easily workable, although one of them, Cae Mochyn, received its name not because the pigs liked rooting around in the field but because towards the bottom it plunged into a horrendously steep gradient down to a brook before flattening out suddenly into a spiteful bog at the water's edge. Other fields were as picturesquely named: Cae Rhwyng Dwy Wal (the field between two walls); Cae Pwll Chi (the field of the dogs' pond); and my favourite, Ton Hywel (Howell's place), the first of Tydraw's fields on the approach over the mountain from Trehafod. To the south the land descends to a delightful wooded dingle with a clear, coruscating mountain brook, ideal for washing sheep. Ample outbuildings, cowsheds, stables, a closed barn with a loft, and pigsties enclosed a cobbled courtyard, and a stone's throw away was a Dutch barn.

A well, always generously supplied with pure mountain water, lay in the field adjoining the house, about twenty yards from the bailey and back kitchen door, and to cap all these delights, from the front of the house lies one of the finest views in Glamorgan, encompassing the village of Penycoedcae and the town of Llantrisant on the left, the wooded Mynydd y Maelog (always known as the Smilog) on the right, and beyond, the sweep of the Vale of Glamorgan, the Bristol Channel with its Flat and Steep Holms, and on fine days, Somerset and Devon. Breathtaking!

The Tydraw land had been farmed during the Napoleonic wars before the house was built. British ships were engaged in battle; there were few available to transport grain; food was scarce; and where land was suitable for growing crops it was brought into use. The idyllic situation impelled some sensible farmer to build a farmhouse on the site. Indeed, about the same time another was built on the land half a mile away and a hundred feet lower down towards Pontypridd: Gelliwion.

Despite their only having four bedrooms and one dressing-room, the Richards family settled in happily, the children sleeping two or

46

three to a room. Hired farm-workers slept in beds on the wide landing. Downstairs were three large rooms: the parlour, where the best pictures, china and hats were kept; the kitchen with its array of pewter and lustre-ware and grandfather clock; and the back kitchen, with its vast fireplace and ceiling-hooks for sides of bacon. The latter and the dairy were the 'engine-rooms' of the whole undertaking, for in these huge amounts of food were prepared for the appetites of farm-workers, cheese, butter, bread and fruit tarts made, pigs salted and hung, clothes cleaned, ironed and repaired, meals taken, newspapers read and children prepared for life. The family got smaller as two brothers died, some of the girls left to be married and one accompanied a brother to work another farm, until only the three youngest children remained and the eldest son, who ran the farm with his father.

The children went to Maesycoed School — a daily walk for them of about four miles — clutching little packets of wholesome food for lunch, a chunk of bread spread with home-made butter together with a piece of farm cheese, a few pickled onions and a piece of fruit cake. The morning walk was downhill, so they were usually on time for class, but dallied on the homeward journey, fascinated by the goings-on at the Maritime Colliery visible from the road, watching the lambs in the fields, gathering hazel-nuts and wild flowers in season and loitering around Gelliwion talking to Mr Williams the farmer before the final haul up to Tydraw.

At twelve years of age my mother transferred to Mill Street Secondary School in Pwllgwaun. This was even further away, involving not only the long walk but a bus ride as well, so despite having a school uniform of which she was inordinately proud, especially a straw boater with a green, white and red band and a silk-embroidered badge disporting an image of the Old Bridge, the arduous journey took its toll in tiredness and after a few years she left school altogether to help her mother on the farm.

When she turned twenty, being a lively girl and wanting to see something of the town, and moreover desiring some financial independence, she took a position as seamstress in the ladies' clothing department of a Pontypridd outfitters. Her job was to alter clothes ladies had bought which didn't fit: hems taken up or let down, seams made larger or smaller, extra button-holes worked in garments and so on. Sometimes people of the wrong shape and size for a piece of clothing accidentally burst a seam or stepped on a hem and my mother had to repair the damage.

Five or six years later an unusual situation occurred which decided my mother to finish paid work and stay at home. Her elder sister, Polly, was married and lived in a small house in Maesycoed with her husband and two children, the elder of whom, Gwilym, aged three, had clearly determined from that very young age that a farmer's life was for him. On one visit to Tydraw, where he undoubtedly enjoyed being the centre of attention and the apple of his grandparents' eye, he declared he wasn't going home ever again. The family naturally assumed that on the morrow, or perhaps even a few days later, he would be crying for his parents and brother, but no, he stayed, and lived in a much refurbished Tydraw until his death seventy years later. Greater love had no man for a place — and who could blame him? He certainly served his faithful apprenticeship on the daily hike to school, returning every day to the farm when he could merely have stepped across the road to his parents' house.

With a young child in the house, her younger sister, Rachel, and their mother, who was increasingly ill with diabetes, found it difficult to cope, so Sal took on the role of surrogate mother and helped bring up her nephew. Seven years after Gwilym's adoption of Tydraw as home my maternal grandmother died. At that time there was no cure for diabetes; her leg became gangrenous and the doctor told her he could save her life only by amputation below the knee. This she refused and prepared to meet her God. Insulin was discovered and available a year later in 1928. My mother, who was now 33, took over the role of mother to the whole family.

Times were poor in the valleys in the 1930s and transport limited, so what more natural than that the mine-workers and valley dwellers should find their pleasures and relaxation on summer weekends in the countryside. People came in their droves up Gelliwion Mountain from the Rhondda as well as from Pontypridd bearing hampers and kettles. The dingle, from below the neighbouring Tylawinder Farm to the beauty spot known as Shoni's Pond below Penrhiw Farm, was like Barry Island on a bank holiday, and it was often difficult to find a free spot to settle down for a picnic. The brook was dammed up at intervals with stones and clods of earth to make little swimming pools, and trout were tickled out of the water and cooked on fires built in stone circles.

Tydraw had people knocking on its door wanting to buy milk for their brookside tea, and others who simply wanted a glass of milk to quench their thirst, sitting on the grass and taking in the magnificent view while resting their feet, dusty and tired from the climb up from Trehafod. Such a one was John Davies.

After one or two visits, for some reason he always felt his throat particularly dry at the curve in the road where Tydraw lay, even when he was driving his little Standard Eight, and also perceived a particular longing for milk, served by a slim, auburn-haired young woman with an upright, almost queenly carriage, a challenging look in grey-green, mischievous eyes and a mouth which curled up at the corners, disappearing into a smile. At first Sallie Richards, though not averse to the idea of marriage, was not impressed with the courtship of my father, a town boy. While in a fairly isolated position in the country, she did not lack social encounters. Neighbouring farmers with their sons visited daily on agricultural business and twice on Sundays the farming community met up at the Capel Annibynwyr (built 1843, rebuilt 1877) at Castellau, near Beddau at the eastern edge of Llantrisant Common. In the chapel vestry, concerts were held and 'dramas' were performed annually, with the farmers turned actors.

So to my father's polite request: "Miss Richards, I wonder whether you would care to accompany me to the cinema one evening?" her instant and peremptory reply was: "Dear me, no. I've got better things to do than that!" Undiscouraged, he would ask a few days later: "Perhaps, Miss Richards, you would like to come for a drive in my car?" This usually impressed the ladies — but not this one. On seeing him approach the house for the glass of milk, she would send Rachel out to serve him. The milk paid for, he would ask: "I wonder if I could speak to the other Miss Richards, if it's not inconvenient?" Sometimes he would leave disappointed, but eventually, firmly believing in the efficacy of 'faint heart ne'er won fair lady', he found his persistence rewarded. On occasions at requests for rendezvous my mother half-teasingly would say: "No, I wasted my time going out with you last week. Ask my sister, Rachel. Why don't you pester her for a change?"

Unfortunately for my father-to-be, he did not have a farm. It was obvious to all that he was not just a milk addict, and the family began to disapprove of his frequent visits. Doubtless they began to talk to my mother in terms of "fly-by-night valley lads", "wide boys", then later of: "fortune-hunters" and "dowry-seekers". Though not rich, they were farmers and clearly not impoverished. After all, my mother, with Rachel, looked after the family and my ageing but still working grandfather considered her indispensable to the smooth running of the farm. John Davies was obviously in love with Sallie Richards, and remained devoted to her for the rest of his life. In fact, a reasonably healthy man all his days, he was destroyed by her death in 1977 and he followed her to the grave a year later.

Two letters were discovered after my father's death, and I hope he and my mother grant me permission *in absentia* to write them here. They are written in typescript but with the envelope addressed in my father's perfect copperplate handwriting:

Dear darling, beloved Sal,

I love you and I'd like you for my wife. Will you marry me? Let's get engaged, shall we? You've known me now for some months (I've known you as many months as you've known me days and I know that I shall always love and worship you) and you should know whether you care enough for me to become my wife.

Should you, as I hope you will, agree to become engaged, I will either write to your father asking an appointment with a view to having his permission, or I will write your younger brother, asking him to be our guest for a day Channel trip, when I will give him particulars relating to myself (credentials, etc). I'd like to meet your brother. Besides, he would probably be able to form an idea as to whether I'd make you a good husband or not.

Perhaps the latter course would be best. Your father might kick me out. Or the excitement entailed in such an interview could possibly have such an adverse effect on his health as to make such an interview undesirable.

Of course I will abide by your decision in the matter. If you would rather defer the engagement until some future time, it's quite all right with me.

But personally I can see no obstacle to prevent us becoming engaged. Neither can I think of one. Unless you don't feel quite sure that you care enough for me.

You can believe me when I say that your happiness comes first and foremost with me. It always will. And if you do decide to get engaged and subsequently meet someone else you'd prefer, well, you would be quite entitled to break with me. But as far as I'm concerned, I'm perfectly and positively sure that I shall never love or marry anyone but You. If I'm not to be the fortunate one, I shall resign myself to being celibate.

Assuring you of my sincere and genuine love and respect, I am

Yours always
Jack

He must have received an unfavourable reply with family talk and criticisms passed on, or no reply at all, for the other letter, altogether more formal, but desperate, is dated a week later, August 23rd, 1934.

Miss Sallie Richards   40 Bryn Eirw
Tydraw Farm   Trehafod
Pontypridd

Dear Sal,

I trust that by now you have digested the contents of the letter I handed you last week.

The synopsis is this: You either decide NOW to get engaged, to marry me at your convenience and arrange to hand your inheritance to either your favourite brother or sister; or divide it between them; or divide it among all the members of your family; or do whatever you like with it; but you are definitely not bringing anything in the form of a dowry to our marriage (if it transpires) (as I hope it will) except your trousseau.

I want to make that quite clear. I love you and want you for my wife and I see no reason why we cannot get engaged now. I love you and want you for yourself, NOT for your inheritance, and if you cannot accept me as I am, if you haven't the courage to get engaged, I think you'd better look out for someone who is prepared to accept an inheritance along with his wife.

Do this. (I mean, get engaged, and tell your people you want nothing in the way of monetary benefit). And I'll wait until your father dies before I expect you to marry me.

Let me know your decision in due course. If it's favourable, I shall be at the usual place on Sunday evening. If it's unfavourable, I shall remain at home

And always be
Yours fraternally
John Davies

51

They were married on a Sunday morning, 11th November 1935, at St David's Church, Gyfeillion, in Hopkinstown, a few miles north of Pontypridd. No one on my mother's side of the family was present at the wedding, clearly showing their disapproval. The wedding car came to fetch her half an hour late, then proceeded to break down outside Gelliwion, where she was delayed for a further hour, while my father, a bag of nerves lest she had changed her mind, waited patiently inside the church with his sister, Mary Ann and cousin, John Thomas, his best man, only too aware that the time for matins was fast approaching.

There was no reception, and they departed immediately afterwards for their honeymoon at the Seabank Hotel in Porthcawl.

John Davies brought his bride, Sallie, to live with his mother behind the shop in Bryn Eirw, and there they lived for the rest of their lives. Their daughter was born there on 6th September 1936 as the bell of St Barnabas's rang out to summon the faithful to evensong.

At first my mother found it difficult to settle down. She was used to the wide open, quiet spaces, empty but for sheep and cows, and here she was in a small terraced house in a narrow valley, in close proximity to a busy colliery, underneath a steep mountain when previously she had been virtually on its summit. What a difference a few miles made! It was another world and she desperately missed her home and her family, although she was welcomed by the friendly Trehafod people, who took an interest in everyone and everything. During the day her husband was at work and she was left in a house not her own with a woman she barely knew, trying to help serve in a grocery shop — a trade quite foreign to her.

On top of this her close family were displeased with her and she worried about her father, who would be missing her — and who could look after him as well as she? It was the worst possible way to start married life.

On the plus side, she had married a most honourable man who adored her. Brought up a good church boy, he did not take lightly promises he made at the altar. Not for nothing had he said: "With my body I thee worship", for he loved her all his life, and: "With all my worldly goods I thee endow" to him meant giving her every penny he ever earned. She controlled the family purse-strings and after my grandmother's death ran the business and paid all the commercial and private bills. I suppose my father was determined to prove she didn't need any of this dowry or inheritance aforementioned and that he had married her purely for love. Although they had their ups and downs, there were certainly never any arguments or quarrels about money or even questions from my father about what she spent money on or why. His trust and love were total.

I often heard her say: "If you make your bed, you've got to lie in it." She heeded this dictum and duly got on with life.

CHAPTER SIX
Gwyn the Milk

One of my earliest memories is of being warm and cosy in my mother's arms, cwtched up against her bosom, a beige-checked Welsh shawl wrapped around both of us.

The side window of our kitchen overlooked the back yard and wash-house, and as the houses were built on a slope we looked up to the neighbours' back gardens. But most of all what my mother's eyes saw was Gelliwion Mountain, which towers above the valley, sheltering Trehafod below it, and doubtless her mind's eye went beyond, over the top, and down the gentler slopes to the family she'd left, wondering how they were in Tydraw.

Sometimes she would point excitedly up at the mountain and say: "Look, Mari fach, look! There's your uncle Dick on his horse after the sheep." For Tydraw sheep grazed Gelliwion Mountain, but look as I might, my baby eyes could never make out what she was pointing at. In later years, though, I saw him straight away, knowing exactly where to look as I became as familiar with the mountain as with my mother's face. Some of my most exciting childhood moments were spent sitting on the horse in front of Uncle Dick, hanging on to the horse's mane as we galloped over the turf and through the ferns, much to my mother's anxiety about my safety.

She had another link with home, though, which she cherished, and that was through Gwyn the Milk. Gwyn Williams lived with his wife, daughter, aged parents and farm boy in Tylawinder, the next farm to Tydraw, not a mile further on. Its land was not as accessible and workable as Tydraw's, being on a steeper, rockier slope, nor its acreage as great, and to eke out the living obtained from the farm, and being the sole support of the family, Gwyn sold milk in Trehafod.

This entailed walking over the mountain no matter what the weather was like every day throughout the year, leading a pony with two churns of milk, one strapped either side of it. The journey was only just over two miles but what miles they were, especially in rain and particularly snow, when the steep, stony mountain path on the Trehafod side had to be negotiated. I never remember his not turning up, although I suppose there must have been times when he didn't make it. I do remember most mornings before leaving for school looking up at the mountain, seeing the dark moving shapes of the little convoy carefully picking its way down the steep gradient, and thinking the school bus would be along in five minutes.

A sturdy, ever cheerful young man, Mervyn, worked for him on Tylawinder, and was a great physical and moral support to Gwyn both on the farm and on the milk. Mervyn was a Williams too, but in this case they were not related.

Gwyn's daily presence in Trehafod was a lifeline to my mother in her early married days, as he brought news in Welsh of her family and, as she eventually discovered, gave them news of her, too, as the heart-ache apparently was not one-sided. Finally, within the year, with Gwyn as go-between, the Richardses forgave their daughter and sister for abandoning them. She went 'home' as she always called it and was welcomed with open arms.

Although Gwyn Tylawinder must have made his daily hike for twenty years, he was far from being an athletic-looking man. Thin and gaunt, dark of hair and eyes, he was bent of frame, never seeming able to stand upright — perhaps the everyday steep mountain haul had permanently forced his body into that forward leaning position. His complexion was ruddy, though, and he looked healthy. His family, father, himself and daughter, had reputations for local *eisteddfodau* successes in the recitation of the Welsh verse form *cynghanedd*, and they were active in the production of the Castellau 'dramas', always performing in them and sometimes writing them.

Gwyn always appeared absorbed in his own thoughts, often with his lips moving slightly, as though talking to himself — no doubt practising for the eisteddfod or the play. To me he didn't look the typical countryman, with an appetite for farming like my uncles. He eventually abandoned the difficulties of working Tylawinder and

55

became a school caretaker in nearby Tonyrefail, where he lived to a good age.

My mother loyally supported Gwyn in his dramas every year, and as my father was no great enthusiast of evening extramural entertainment (apart from a ritual Saturday night outing to the Llanover Arms in Pontypridd), for he'd been working all day at the test-beds, it was I who accompanied my mother to the play.

"Mary'll go with you, Sal. I'll mind the shop and have a nice cup of tea waiting for you when you get home."

I don't remember much about the performances, except that the tiny chapel vestry was packed and almost everyone knew my mother and greeted her warmly. Former neighbours from the surrounding farms, the Miles of Penbwch, Evans Gellidraws and the Davieses of Llwynau, would kiss and hug her with cries of "Sal Tydraw! Well, well, how are you? Haven't seen you for such a long time!" as though she were the long-lost princess of a tribe.

I do nevertheless remember the performance we had getting there. First, down to the Vaughan's Arms and wait there for a Ponty bus. That part of the trip undertaken, we had to make our way up the Tumble in Pontypridd to the Beddau bus queue behind the white building of the County Cinema, where often I would have preferred to go. This bus was an ancient, rickety single-decker that appeared to tour South Wales before arriving at Beddau. Finally there was a mile walk from the Gelynog Inn down to Castellau Chapel, where a collection of saddled horses would be tethered to the sign-post opposite the Lamb and Flag (*Yr Oen a'r Faner*) and gambos with horses and tractors with trailers parked at the roadside. Our long journey meant that we normally sat at the back of the vestry, and while I could hear very well what was going on I couldn't see much apart from black-overcoated shoulders and the silhouettes of ears, hair and hats. My mother always enjoyed the outing though, but I had a sneaking suspicion she went for the interval rather than the play.

Mervyn, who was the antithesis of Gwyn, hail and hearty, well-built and strong, was like Paddy Collins — he could only shout. You knew the moment the milk reached the Tump, and from inside the house could follow its delivery progress through the streets. This was useful, as if you had an imminent appointment elsewhere you could take your jug to the exact place where Mervyn would be, get it filled and depart with no fear of missing the day's delivery.

He would stride into our house past the shop, slamming the door, bawling: "Milk, Mrs Davies, milk!" My mother would wince but not say anything. What was the point? Thousands had said to him: "Don't shout so loud, Mervyn, I'm not deaf" and he would grin generously, showing a mouthful of beautiful teeth in his ruddy, weatherbeaten face and carry on just as before.

He had a heart of gold and would run and fetch, for old people especially. Nothing was too much trouble for him and despite his vocal energy everybody loved him. In later years he learned to drive and Gwyn bought a Morris Minor van, Mervyn's pride and joy, in which to ferry them and the milk from Tylawinder. Mervyn was far from being an intellectual like Gwyn, and while he had no difficulty in learning the mechanics of driving, he had difficulty, like so many other people, myself included, in instant reaction to left and right. My father would keep reminding him when they discussed driving in the house: "Right foot, accelerator and brake; left foot, clutch, Mervyn. And your right foot is on the same side as the hand you write with." However Mervyn was not without imagination. As he delivered the milk on the day of his driving test, we saw he had something white on his black shoes. Closer examination revealed he had painted a C on the toe of his left shoe and a B and an A on the right one. He grinned widely and showed us, to great amusement, the backs of his hands. On his writing hand he had inked a small R, and an L was marked on the other. Whether he passed his test at that time I can't remember, but he deserved to for initiative.

CHAPTER SEVEN
Home Life

Although our lives were essentially and inextricably bound up with the shop, we did have an existence much like other people in the neighbourhood, except that life in the Davies household was probably busier — it certainly was never boring. As for everyone else, or probably because everyone else did the same, and therefore couldn't go shopping, Monday was wash-day. Apart from an early-morning run on Fairy washing soap, Lux soap flakes and Persil or Rinso washing powder, things were fairly quiet. A fire would be lit in the grate in the wash-house and a huge aluminium bucket of water was put on to boil. The dirty clothes, with washing powder over them, were placed in a wooden tub, and when the water was ready the whole lot was attacked by Mam wielding a 'dolly' (a thick wooden wheel with crenellations on the underside, fixed to a handle with a cross-bar at the top) with which she battered the poor clothes, turning and pummelling them as she vigorously moved and twisted the dolly around in the tub. It was a very energetic performance and I assumed her weekly after-dinner nap on Sundays was to build up her reserves of strength for the Monday washing activities.

There was steam and water everywhere, no less on Mam's sweating brow, and by the end of the day, her curls had all gone. The more recalcitrant clothes would remain for further punishment while the clean ones were wrung out and put aside for later attentions. Now a washing board — a flat piece of wood with a little shelf at the top for the soap and a ribbed piece of yellow metal covering the surface — would appear and the torture of the clothes continue. These poor sufferers were rarely mine (unless I'd been sitting on rusty pipes!) but my father's working shirts and dungarees. After soap had been applied, they were mercilessly rubbed up and down the metal ribbing until they came clean.

The next ordeal was the rinsing. The soapy, dirty water was discarded — the tub upturned after a struggle — and after meandering all over the back yard found its way to the drain. More buckets of hot water, more cold from the tap, more dollying and hey, presto! the clothes were clean.

Before the wringing, my mother would have a cup of tea and get her second wind, for this was the worst job of all, where the clothes got their revenge. She would take each garment in her poor, reddened, water-wrinkled hands and twist it as hard as she could. Surprisingly she managed to squeeze out most of the water, but when I tried even handkerchiefs defeated me. After white items had been dipped in starch solution, the clothes were hung up on the wire line above the garden path, with little two-legged wooden pegs with round heads, and the whole thing propped up with a long wooden pole with a V cut out at one end. The clothes would dance and flutter in the wind, joyful at their release from captivity and admonishment, and my mother would stand looking at them for a few seconds, pleased with her efforts and, I'm sure, relieved it was over for another week.

Right up the street everyone's back garden would be garlanded with drying clothes, swinging on lines like triumphant flags proclaiming the Battle of Washday had been won.

It was no surprise that every spare moment of Tuesday, once the ironing was done, was given over to repairs to the beaten and battered garments.

After the war my mother had a most marvellous invention, a mangle, also useful for pressing flowers, and fingers too if you weren't careful. Subsequently a washing machine, with its own electric dolly, not to mention an electric mangle, arrived on the scene, eventually to be replaced by a two-drum machine that would even partially dry the clothes itself. Finally, of course, came the automatic, and nobody had to do anything except twiddle a few knobs and flick a switch. But wash-day was never the same.

Every Wednesday was market-day in Pontypridd and at about ten o'clock my mother would shut the shop for the morning and, be-hatted, sally forth down Bryn Eirw Hill armed with a shopping-basket to catch the Ponty bus outside the Vaughan's Arms. Before long the familiar, friendly-looking double-decker would round the colliery bend, and the shoppers who had been to Porth would step or jump off with smiles, jokes and greetings, making room for the new passengers. Elderly ladies were usually given a helping hand and uttering 'Oooh's and 'Aaah's were lifted off or hauled up onto the step by the conductor, who had straps criss-crossing his chest, one attached to his stiff, leather bag containing fares, and the other to the ticket-machine. This held half a dozen or so tickets, differently coloured depending on destination and whether the ride was single or return.

Depressing a little lever on the top of the machine would release the cardboard ticket, which was then punched and handed to the passenger with a little square hole in it. A return ticket had to be stowed away carefully in purse or pocket, but was nevertheless frequently lost.

I suppose there were time-tables for these buses, but they were so frequent at ten minute intervals people never bothered to consult them, so it was annoying to be halfway down Bryn Eirw Hill and see the yellow and blue one with P.U.D.C and a representation of the old bridge painted on its side just departing down Sant's Hill. However, the maroon version with R.U.D.C on it would be along soon. The arrival of buses for Porth was more easily espied from the top of Church Hill, as you could see them approaching along Phillips Terrace from the Rhondda Bridge bus stop at the Non-Pol, and with a quick downhill sprint you could beat the bus to its stop as it toiled, fuming when laden, up Sant's Hill. My father preferred Porth while my mother barely knew of its existence. Pontypridd was her Mecca. My loyalties were divided between both.

My mother didn't really need to travel to Pontypridd every Wednesday as there was nothing we required that was unobtainable in Trehafod, but it was a little like the 'dramas' — a social occasion — and what better excuse for an outing?

She loved the bustle and hubbub of the stalls on Market Square and bought things she didn't want, perhaps because of the persuasive tongue of a salesman with a twinkle in his eye or perhaps because it was a bargain and 'would come in useful' at some future time. Mam couldn't resist lengths of material — "I've bought a nice bit of stuff today" — and we also had a large collection of towels, pillow-cases, sheets; variously sized pots and pans; fish spatulas, vegetable mashers and ingenious devices for chopping herbs that took ages to assemble and trapped the fingers; pastry crimpers, chip-cutters, egg-slicers; scissor-like devices for cutting tomatoes into pretty shapes; butter-curlers and sieves of all sizes from tea-strainers up. Shopping-days were always interesting.

"What's this evil-looking contraption for, Sal?" my father would ask as my mother's basket was unloaded.

"Oh, no, you've got it upside down, look, Jack. It's for grating cheese or carrots. You put the cheese in there, see, on top of this little wheel and... Ooops-a-daisy!"

At this point my mother would dive after some part of the implement that had become dislodged and rolled off under the table. The part retrieved, my mother would continue with the instructions for use, and my father would finish with a puzzled:

"Oh. I see. Very good."

Then the little machine would be put in the table drawer, only to see the light of day when the latter was emptied for cleaning once a year.

After Market Square, it was up the Arcade, past the Co-op Clothing, Footwear and Hairdressers' shops at the bottom end, to call in to say hullo on Olwen Williams, formerly of Hargroves Clothiers of Taff Street, who now kept her own fashion shop at the top of the Arcade opposite the police station. Then around the corner, past Oswald Davies the Chemists, fittingly positioned opposite Crawford the dentist in Market Street, and into the meat market to buy Dad's dinners for the week from Ralph Perkins and his merry band of joking meat-men.

"Oh, Mrs Davies! Late today. Been gossiping again? I dunno, you women, gossip, gossip, gossip. And we men work..."

"Oh, come on, Don. No time for silly nonsense today, or I'll miss my sister. Three nice lamb chops, a bit of brisket, and I'll have four or five slices of that pig's liver over by there."

The meat was paid for, some bloody change handed to my mother, although Don constantly wiped his hands on his white apron; more light-hearted chat and mother would be off, dodging through a narrow passage-way past the materials stall to another part of the market and to Plowman's fish stall to buy the hake for that evening's dinner.

If it was a Saturday morning and I was with her, my appealing, thirsty gaze as we passed the pop stall a bit further on from Perkins's would prompt her to buy me a glass of Tizer in the summer or hot blackcurrant when the weather was cold. On Saturdays, too, she would buy chitterling from Lemmie Griffiths's stall for my father's post-pub supper, and Lemmie would give me a bit of black pudding to chew.

I liked accompanying my mother to the market on Saturdays, but with the crowds and shopping baskets and manipulating money and purses, having a small girl to look after as well, especially one who dragged her to the secondhand book and comic stall, to the biscuit stall, sweet stall, toy stall and especially the engraver's stall, must have been a trial for her, but I never had a smack and never heard a word of complaint from her. The engraver's little stall was at the end of the meat market. He sold rings, bangles, necklaces and dog-collars with a flat part on them, some an inch or so long, on which to engrave the owner's name. This he did with a metal tool like a pencil on the end of a curly wire, and as he engraved on the metal, with what looked like an eye-bath fixed in one eye, the pencil hummed as he wrote. We had bought a collar from him for our dog, Peter, and not only did he have his name but his address around his neck as well. This perhaps was a little supererogatory, as a great adventure to Peter was putting just his nose outside the door to acknowledge the day before immediately returning to the comfort of the mat in front of the fire.

To my pleading, my mother bought me a silver ring and in fascination we watched an M being engraved on it. I only wanted the ring for the engraving, and it was quite good value, as the initial lasted twelve years before fading into illegibility.

Sometimes as we wandered through the market I would reach for my mother's hand and walk along, chatting away, then look up for her response, a smile, or agreement or otherwise and to my horror see a stranger's face — always with an amused expression — and I would mumble some apology after biting my lower lip or putting a flustered hand to my round, open mouth, then, on tiptoe, frantically look all around. Mam would be looking at the woollen stall, quite unaware of my adopting a passer-by, or walking behind me, having a little chuckle as she watched me.

One day when aged five I really did get lost. During the time we kept chickens, Mam had to go to Caddy's animal food stores just below the Collier's Arms pub in Mill Street to buy them grain. As they knew the Richards family, this visit was always a long drawn out affair and I would seek some diversion to pass the time, often going into the store-room to examine the various sacks of meal, grain, dog biscuits, cattle food and birdseed. When I thought we'd been there long enough, I emerged — but my mother was nowhere to be seen.

"Oh, there you are, Mary. Your mother's been looking for you everywhere. She thought you must have gone to the market and she went looking for you."

Hoping I'd catch her up, I ran for dear life down Mill Street and up past Marenghi's café on the corner, and the arcade, to the market. Naturally in the crowds it was like looking for a cat in a corn-field. Trembling lip and chin burst into a trickle of tears. How was I going to get home on the bus? My mother had my ticket and I had no money in my pocket.

As people began to notice me crying, I felt self-conscious and mopped up my tears on my sleeve. After all, if I didn't find my mother, Ralph Perkins or Olwen Williams would lend me tuppence for the bus, or even Mr Crawford, the dentist, outside whose surgery I was standing — but I didn't really want to bother him. So there was truly no need to cry, and after all, I knew where the bus-stop was.

I decided on a plan of action. I might as well enjoy myself since I was lost, so I'd go down the park, spend some time there on the swings and slide, then come back to the bus-stop outside Woolworth's and wait there for my mother, when she'd finished her shopping, to come and catch the bus home.

There were a few kids in Ynysangharad Park running round unaccompanied, and I got on the roundabout with some. We took it in turns to run round holding on to the metal bars and pushing, then jumping onto the running board and sliding onto the slatted seat section.

"Do you live in Ponty, little girl?"

"No, I'm from Trehafod. I'm lost."

"This is in Ponty Park."

"I know."

"Well, you're not lost, then."

"Yes, I am. My mother's lost me, in Ponty."

"Oh. Are you going home after?"

"I can't. I haven't got any money for the bus."

By this time I was the centre of attention of three or more children. One wanted to take me to someone she called 'the Parkie', another wanted to take me to look for my mother at the baths, a place she was most unlikely to be, and another offered to put me up for the night. This last one sounded the most promising, as she also said she had an uncle who was a bus driver, and he would drive me home for nothing in his bus.

Time passed with more plans and suggestions being made, when a policeman strode towards the group of children. Before he could say anything, the one who was going to be my hostess for the night said: "There's a lost girl here, mister. Have you come to fetch her?"

He had, of course, my frantic mother having run around Ponty, the market, the square, the arcade, back to Caddy's, and then, at her wit's end, to the police station. I was quite sorry to leave my new friends in the park. Being lost wasn't so bad and I was rather looking forward to being driven home in the uncle's bus. However, I made sure I clutched the policeman's hand all the way back to the station where my distraught mother was having a cup of tea. Her basket was empty apart from the chicken feed, and that week all our provisions did come from the Trehafod shops.

On Wednesdays, after looking around the vegetable market, which extended as far as Penuel Lane, her purchases made, Mam would double back to the centre of the market, where she would meet her sister, Polly, and they would partake of faggots and peas in the little glass-sided café near the engraver's stall just inside the entrance next to the Town Hall. There, sitting on benches and eating their faggots and peas from bowls on trestle-tables, they would catch up on family and other news and sip strong tea from generous cups. Faggots and peas were always in great demand by shoppers, so if the meal was over before the news the two sisters would depart to leave room for others, and make their way back past the New Inn, Woolworth's and the road to Ynysangharad Park to the Bracchi's on the Tumble for a cup of coffee. The chat and coffee concluded till the following Wednesday, Mam would have a quick nip around Marks and Spencer's to buy me socks or vests, and always one of their hot dogs, before joining the queue for the bus ride home.

People always knew when my mother had been to Ponty because she kept her hat on for the rest of the day, not taking it off until bedtime. Perhaps it was her way of extending her enjoyable day, perhaps it was because she'd taken so long manoeuvring the hatpins into place she wanted to have maximum use of the hat, perhaps it was because her hair was flattened and not as pretty as usual. Whatever the reason, the hat always reminded me on my home-coming from school that there was a cold hot dog waiting for me somewhere in the house.

Probably because of her farm upbringing, my mother liked having animals about the place, and from a baby I remember cats and a dog in the house and chickens in the small garden. My mother's attitude to pets, though, was quite different from that of most village people. They were there for a purpose as far as she was concerned.

There were a lot of cats in the neighbourhood, all of which seemed to be called Tibby, though for a time I thought some were called Scat, as this is what Mam or my grandmother shouted to them if they came down our steps or walked on the wash-house roof leaving their smell. Our two were both called Puss. One was a large, mainly white and black cat with a very indolent, not to say somnolent look, and the second a small tortoiseshell with a mean eye and a spiteful nature. All they seemed to exist for was food and whenever someone went into the pantry, which was a separate little building outside and opposite the back kitchen door, on hearing the door-latch rattle both cats would magically appear from nowhere, mewing and demanding something to eat; and White and Black Puss would rub against your legs and get in the way. At bed-time when one of them was required to spend the night in the shop with a tray of ashes, you could stand rattling the pantry latch for ages and calling 'Puss!' before one of them would arrive in its own good time, rolling its hips as it ambled along. It would give you a haughty, inquiring look: 'Yes? What do you want?'

Our cats were rarely petted. If my mother saw me pick one up to hold and nurse, she would say: "*Ach y fi*! Put it down, Mary. Cats have fleas" and, reminded of the horror of creepy-crawlies, I would hastily let it drop to the floor. Neither puss wished for petting anyway, it seemed, as they would wriggle and squirm in your grasp, then before springing away give a final dig of a claw into a bit of soft flesh.

The Tortoiseshell Puss must have lived with us solely because it was 'a good mouser', because in every other way it really was more of a nuisance than a help. It kept having kittens, for which homes had to be found (and, dare I say it, for some the 'home' turned out to be a bucket of water). I carried many in cardboard boxes over to Tydraw, for is it not well known there are rats and mice on farms? And voles in fields? And cats are needed? At the continual appearance of these cardboard boxes, my uncle Dick would say: "Duw, duw, more cats? You think I got a cat farm here, do you?" but would let them stay none the less. They were rarely seen again in any case. Tydraw cats were wild, and although food and water was put out for them they had the freedom of the farm and hunted their own food which was in plentiful supply.

Apart from its arrogance, Tortoiseshell Puss would stalk around in dark places under people's feet. If you trod on its tail or feet, or even came too close, it would emit a blood-curdling screech, and out would flash its claws to sink into the nearest ankle, shin or calf and draw blood. More often than not it was Mam, as she was the busiest and most mobile in the house, but everyone had their turn. "Hell's bells!" my mother would exclaim, mopping up streaming blood with a hankie, "That damn cat's spagged me again!"

If visitors were expected, the pantry latch was rattled and my mother would croon sweetly: "Puss! Puss! Come on, puss. Milk, milk! There's a good puss." As it was daytime they would arrive post-haste, demanding food. Then my mother would swoop on Tortoiseshell Puss, grab it by the scruff and, sweet tones abandoned, say: "Got you, you devil!" and imprison the growling animal out of the way in the cellar for the afternoon.

My father preferred dogs and, when a single man, always kept a big, virile animal to walk the mountain with him and guard the shop — not that it needed guarding in those days, as there were few villains about.

After they were married my parents had a black spaniel named Peter, and I grew up with him for the first ten years of my life. He was the very antithesis of a guard dog with his appealing brown eyes, long, silky ears and his sweet, timorous nature. He knew how to bark, but forgot to most of the time. The only occasion we heard him making anything approaching a loud noise was when other dogs were involved in a scrap. He would pad off to the street to see what all the fuss was about, watch the furiously twisting, struggling, yapping pair from a safe distance, and give one bark. If the fighting dogs moved down-street closer to him, he would turn tail and bound another twenty yards away, then stand and watch again and give another bark.

He liked best of all to lie on the mat in front of the fire and the family got used to taking a wider, higher step at a certain place. Unlike Tortoiseshell Puss, if you accidentally stepped on him he would give a little yelp and, lest he had frightened you with the noise, give your leg a rough-tongued lick.

Peter loved walking, running and playing on the mountain but was always happiest when someone was with him. When out on his own 'to do his business' as Mam or Gran euphemistically said, he would return with the minimum of delay. He didn't like the ponds however and according to my father couldn't swim. When a puppy he had been thrown into Coedcae pond by one of the tough men and had needed rescuing. Perhaps he had been caught in some weeds, perhaps he had been too small for such an experience. Whatever, the only water he liked was that in his bowl to be drunk.

He would sit on his haunches well away from the pond as I played ducks and drakes or leaned over the water watching and fishing for tiddlers in jam jars, and the boys mocked: "Aaah! Look at Mary Davies's hopeless dog. He can't swim. He's afraid of the water. Let's chuck him in!"

Don't you dare! I'll get my father on to you!"

And knowing my father was quite liable to jump over the counter and give a cheeky boy a quick clip around the ear to sort him out, they desisted. They wouldn't have been able to catch Peter anyway, as he ran for dear life away from water.

He wasn't any good at jumping up and catching balls in flight in his mouth as many lithe mongrel dogs could, but he was able to retrieve a thrown stick, provided of course it wasn't thrown into water, and he was happy to go on doing this all day, panting happily and furiously wagging his tail as though he were in line for the gold medal at Cruft's.

He was a pedigree dog, and we assumed most of the intelligence and aggression had been bred out of him, leaving only amiability and sweetness of disposition.

Just inside the door leading into the house from the shop was the staircase giving access to the bedrooms. Next to that another door gave onto the living room, and here stood two objects, the piano, my father's pride, and the book-case, his joy.

The black ebony piano, made by Kaps of Dresden, had been acquired in Bath and its iron frame was so heavy it had gone through the floor of the removal van bringing it to Trehafod. In the living room it stood against the wall, its weight distributed with its wheels resting on thick, brown glass concave objects that looked like heavy ash-trays. Ornate brass candle-holders, two on each side, extended out beyond the keyboard so that a romantic candlelight evening with music and song could be enjoyed, or, if not that, piano practice could continue during a power cut. The trouble with the candles was that as they burned lower, the grease would tend to miss the holder, especially if the candle was slightly askew or ill-fitting, and, while it also missed the ivory keys, a bare arm would sometimes come in for hot wax treatment, occasioning a howl fit to ruin any romantic evening. Swinging around like a professional musician, eyes closed when transported by the music, was hazardous, too, since you tended to bump your head on one of the candlesticks and come to a sudden, inelegant and painful stop.

My father played when he was kept waiting, ready to go out, dressed in a suit, stiff collar and tie and wearing gleaming shoes. It might be a bank holiday trip to Porthcawl or even Tydraw or another relative's farm, or a shopping expedition to Cardiff, or the annual church outing to Barry Island. Whatever it was, Dad was always ready to go ages before Mam, who had to wash, change, dress, make up and bejewel herself and finally close the performance with the great ritual of the putting on of the hat. Dad, pacing about downstairs, would say: "Go and see if your mother's ready, or what stage she's at in her dressing!" and if I reported back that she had not yet put her hat on, he would sigh and mutter: "Oh, a good half-hour yet, then", and to my delight move towards the piano.

He usually played without music and always started with *The Robin's Return*, a highly impressive piece with lots of pretty trills and scale-type passages which required mastery of technique and sureness of touch — at least, so it seemed compared to my Grade One piano-plonking ability. The shop-window blind would be down in readiness to close up shop in our absence, but unaware customers would arrive nonetheless. At such times I hated their disturbing the performance and I would go glowering to serve them, while simultaneously strutting with pride at their hearing my father's expertise. I would run upstairs to delay my mother's preparations, perhaps hiding the gloves which she always wore, lacy ones in summer, leather in winter. She would say: "Mari fach, go and fetch the blue hat-pin from the jug on the dresser, there's a good girl." Hat-pin hidden, I would shout quietly up the stairs, so as not to disturb my father at the piano: "Can't find it, Mam", and this ploy always ensured another ten minutes' delay.

Mam would consult me about the tidiness of her hair under the hat.

"No, it's all sticking out at different levels at the back. You'll have to do it again."

Father went through his delightful Strauss repertoire, then the Barcarolle from *The Tales of Hoffman,* then a bit of *Il Trovatore,* and when he started on Handel's *Largo,* I knew the performance was winding down. He always finished with the beautiful *Maiden's Prayer,* a lilting, haunting, romantic piece composed by someone of the name of Thecla Baderewska, so I would rush from wherever I was to watch him play, as this required the 'hands across' technique which I thought the height of skill and mastery. How I longed to be able gracefully to swoop my left hand over my right and with a flourish hit the right note, withdraw, then do it again! Of course I always had to be there at the conclusion to give a final round of applause to encourage him to play again before the next outing. My father would smile at my enthusiasm, then sigh deeply and say: "Oh, God! Isn't she ready yet?"

Having been formerly employed as a bookseller, my father naturally had a lot of books. As his taste and experience were liberal, these ranged from the great classics of literature: Thackeray, Jane Austen, Walter Scott, Defoe, Dumas, Poe, Kingsley, Reade, Mrs Gaskell, and Hardy through tomes of mining engineering down to *The Universal Book of Hobbies and Handicrafts* and various manuals on

Swimming Made Easy, Driving Made Easy and so on. All the books were in more or less new condition and were kept behind glass in a large book-case against the staircase wall. I don't remember him as much of a reader, although he daily read every word of the *Western Mail* and got through three newspapers on Sunday. He was busy most of the time, for after coming home from his carpentry job at six o'clock he took over the shop from my mother and did all the business accounting as well. He repaired the house himself and also made wooden objects in the workshop he had set up in the former bakehouse in the back garden, so there wasn't much time for reading.

To me the book-case was a real Pandora's box (but in this case of treasures). High up on the top shelf (probably because it was the nearest point to God) and way out of reach was kept every Welsh family's major work, *Y Bibl*, sporting a metal clasp, and in which were recorded the births of ancestors dating back through the last century. Next to the bible were two of the largest dictionaries I had ever seen, with finger indentations to help you find the right page. Meanings were detailed in explanation and there were finely drawn black and white illustrations as well. When I unlocked the book-case's glass doors and took a chair to reach and explore its contents, my mother would say: "Be careful, Mary. For God's sake, don't touch those books high up. If they fell on top of you, they'd crush you." And she wasn't joking, for they were monsters.

I suppose I felt most proud of the classics. There were two rows of them, a complete set of Dickens and all the major great novels and they stood smartly, all the same size, side by side like soldiers in delicately mottled brown vellum uniforms with their titles lettered in gold. It was a pity to remove them for reading, though like good soldiers, so used were they to standing firm that they did not lurch over when one was taken from its place. In later years, when I did attempt to read my way through the classics, I found these particular soldiers with their stiff covers, small print and endless pages unyielding, unwieldy and unfriendly, and the novel was always, after the first few pages, completed in a much thumbed, flexible, library version in which you weren't ashamed to turn the page corner down to keep your place.

The other shelves contained various tomes such as the *Harmsworth Self-Educator,* the *Odham's Press Encyclopaedia* in ten or twelve volumes, and one dear little *Pear's Cyclopaedia* for 1928 with the silver image of a shilling embossed on its cover. There was of course a complete Shakespeare, its fine pages inter-leaved with photographs of Sarah Bernhardt, dressed as a man with a sad expression, hand to brow looking into the distance, Henry Irving in declamatory pose and tight trousers, and Ellen Terry encumbered with flowing robes, large, floppy hat and a pair of scales. Pages of tracing paper originally protecting these photographic plates were later removed by a foolish, childish hand for the purpose of tracing secret society badges and shibboleths.

Besides the very tedious, to my mind, volumes on mining engineering there were books scarcely less boring, as for instance *Great Parliamentary Speeches from Burke to Churchill* and *The Complete* (and incomprehensible)*Musical Educator* in five volumes, and a book of long quotations, many in dead or foreign languages, gathered together by a Reverend James Wood.

There was a cupboard at the bottom of the book-case which was separated from the book-shelves by two drawers. Periodicals and art magazines were stored there. These were much pored over as they were reachable without the aid of a chair. In fact, when the doors were open, the magazines tumbled out onto the mat, and a child could simply sit, legs outstretched in a triangular pen formed by the doors, and gaze at the Fighting Temeraire, Salisbury Cathedral, the Corn Field, the Grand Canal of Venice and various nymphs in ponds, in undress other than flowers in their hair, and in different poses, draped over rocks or the bank, paddling or coyly feeling the water but never swimming. The alternative to this was the popular *Illustrated Story of the Nations* in fifty weekly parts, price 7d per week. Whether all fifty parts were in residence, I don't know, but it was the covers that appealed to me most — there were old-fashioned pictures inside and a lot of tiny writing — as the title of each one was printed in a different shade. I didn't know so many colours existed. The greens ranged from pale aqua through sage to deep forest green, and similarly with the other colours, the browns starting at pale coffee and reaching rich, dark chocolate.

All my father's ties were kept in one of the drawers and these were a source of great delight to me with their varied colours, patterns and materials and little tabs underneath saying where they had been bought: Oliver Howell, Menswear Outfitters, Hannah Street,

Porth; Hodges and Sons, Taff Street, Pontypridd; Earnest (sic) Jones, Bon Ton, Pontypridd. I loved to play with them, constantly assuring those passing that I was tidying and straightening them as their home was a cardboard box from the shop which, though it had contained licorice strips, was still far too short to house a whole length of tie without its being folded at least once. I loved the smell of my father's ties as I did that of his clothes. It was the aroma of the outside, adult men's world, tobacco, shaving cream, leather, wood and his own personal smell, quite easily identifiable from anyone else's.

In the other drawer was a box containing dozens of stiff white collars of various shapes, but, initial curiosity satisfied, these were relatively uninteresting objects and, as each was stored inside the next, withdrawal of one was a nuisance, as the circle closed tighter and you couldn't get the collar back in without a great deal of trouble.

Apart from the hymn and prayer books, including my favourite one with an ivory cover bearing a silver cross which I usually examined during sermons, and packets of dull legal documents, such as house deeds, relatives' wills and papers to do with ground rents using terms such as leasehold and freehold, words I didn't understand or find interesting, that was it.

Among the books I had three favourites. One was a brown, leather-bound, manageable copy of *The People's Encyclopaedia*, and I loved it mainly for the coloured pages inserted at intervals showing species of tree, breeds of dog, types of fish, different precious and semi-precious stones, butterflies, ships, fungi and so it went on. My view of the perfect book was one entirely made up of such colourful illustrated pages, without the load of small print, explanations and polysyllabic words that most such books consisted of.

Another much looked-at book was a pictorial history of the first thirty years of the Twentieth Century. It contained many sepia photographs throughout of the royal family — various kings on ships who all looked alike with little pointed beards, wearing admiral's uniforms, unsmiling kings and queens and miserable-looking princes and princesses posing for formal photographs, waving from balconies or striding through lines formed by policemen wearing hip-length belted jackets and holding back crowds of people who all waved little flags. There were various politicians: Mr Churchill being shot at in the siege of Sydney Street, and Mr Lloyd George scurrying along wearing a cloak and looking worried, Mrs Pankhurst making a speech on a wooden box and another suffragette running in front of a race-horse. Then there was a fine young American woman in a bathing suit and with a towel round her shoulders who had swum the Channel; the French tennis player, Jean Borotra, wearing cricket trousers; and a golfer wearing not only strange, puffed out check trousers but a ridiculous checked flat cap as well. Soldiers in desperate situations and poses abounded, but I skipped through the war, preferring the postwar photographs of people on beaches, the ladies in 'daring' costumes — at least, so the caption said, though why, I couldn't imagine — and the men with striped vests above their bathing trunks. There were photographs of open-topped London buses with their stair-cases on the outside and advertisements for Swan Matches, and fragile-looking aeroplanes piloted by men in open cockpits wearing leather bathing-caps, goggles and streaming scarves.

The other preferred book was my father's oft-consulted *Universal Family Doctor and Medical Adviser (Illustrated)*. My parents, seeing me looking so often at this learned compendium, must have nurtured hopes of my entering the medical profession, but nothing was further from my mind. I wasn't at all keen on blood, boils, pus, phlegm, grazed knees and the like. I looked at it not only because it had photographs and drawings of people's insides, hospital treatment machines and strange complaints like exophthalmic goitres, claw and club feet, gouty big toe, alopoecia and sebacious cysts, but also because on two different pages there were pictures of a naked woman, back and front, and a similarly naked man, though disappointingly the front view of the man had him clothed in a tiny pair of blue underpants. They were well separated, being at either end of the book, as it would doubtless have been rude to depict them on adjoining pages. There were lines drawn to various parts of their bodies and a legend at the bottom of the page told you what you could be suffering from in that particular region. You can imagine my mother's surprise when I, at about nine years of age, announced to her one day, having a slight stomach ache and not wanting to go to school and after of course consulting the *Home Doctor*, that I thought I had a gastric ulcer, or possibly a hernia.

"Dear me! We'd better get you to the hospital straight away, then," was her reply in unanguished tones as I was sent on my way sucking a Rennie.

I could easily understand the *Home Doctor* and thought its information might quite likely be useful one day. For example, under the heading 'Dislocated Jaw' I read that "a yawn may put the lower jaw out of joint". (Oh dear! Early to bed in future, and no reading with a torch under the bedclothes...) "Remove false teeth and go to or send for a doctor to reduce dislocation." Blisters on the feet could be avoided if you heeded the important warning that "no seam should be in the foot of stockings to be worn for a long tramp. Knots and lumps in the wool should be teased out before wearing." I read that "Bleeders or haemophiliacs should be protected in every possible way and trained in some such occupation as that of a clerk or shop-keeper". I was a little worried by this, but soon remembered that my father was also a carpenter. The book went on to tell the story of the poor bleeder kindly employed by his sympathetic doctor to look after the latter's car. Driving it was considered too risky. However the clumsy fellow broke a headlamp, cut his finger and bled to death despite having his doctor nearby. A cautionary tale indeed! Blood pressure of various heights I had heard talk of in the shop and I tried to remember the information for the next victim. "General health must be watched and constipation avoided, a small dose of Epsom salts being taken every morning and a calomel pill once a week." Whether the advice was for high or low blood pressure though I never could remember.

One phrase to do with ill health I kept overhearing in the shop and sometimes in the house was on the matter of change.

"Oh, poor Mrs Webber next door's been bad again. Crying all day yesterday she was, very depressed. On the change, see."

Or in the middle of a chat, a lady customer would say: "Oh, dear me, I must go and have a breath of fresh air by the door. These hot flushes!"

"On the change, are you, Maud?"

"Aye, gul, unfortunately, and it goes on so long, don' it? I dunno, men don' know how lucky they are not to 'ave to go through these things, do they?"

What could this possibly mean, 'on the change'? Were these ladies addicted to the penny falls in the fair, which needed a lot of pennies in change? Were they conductresses on buses, rushing round with change? That would explain the heat. But as far as I knew, they were housewives and didn't have jobs. It couldn't mean they were slowly changing into something else, such as a rabbit or a leopard? No, that was just a silly fairy story.

The mystery continued for some time, but not obsessively, until one day, looking in the *Home Doctor*, I happened to notice the phrase "the change of life" under 'Menopause'. I certainly hadn't heard that word before. So it did have something to do with men after all! But those ladies said men didn't catch it...

I read on. It started in old women of forty-five and ended when they were elderly, at fifty-five. And they couldn't bear children any more. This was more and more puzzling. Old ladies seemed to like me all right. In fact old ladies seemed to like children more than young ones did. I began to fear not only for myself but for my mother when I read: "The tendency to put on flesh at this time is distressing to many women and this increase in weight is accompanied by dryness of the skin, falling out of the hair, dulling of the intelligence and slowing of the heart's action."

I was now feeling hot and depressed myself. I didn't want a shrivelled-up, bald, dense, slow-moving mother who couldn't bear me.

However, even worse was to follow. There was something about periods stopping. Was this to do with periodical magazines similar to those my mother took, I wondered. Then came the awful words which put fear into my heart: "Some women feel greatly increased sexual desire" (didn't know what that was) "and in some cases become unable to control their emotions. These women may be such a nuisance that they have to be shut up in institutions where they can be cared for by specially trained nurses. Their behaviour may cause the break-up of a hitherto happy home."

Well, they certainly weren't taking my mother to an institution when she had increased sexual desire, no hair left and couldn't read her magazines any more. I and my father would see to that! And off I went, indignantly, to tell her so.

I wasn't prepared for her shocked, amazed and angry reaction, being told I was a naughty girl and sent to my room.

No doubt an examination of the apposite pages in the book I'd been reading was soon under way. Shortly I was forgiven and all was more or less well again. In fact, my mother even seemed rather amused now. It was then I learned about the problems confronting a lady in her life.

No matter which Trehafod house you entered — and this was probably the case throughout the Rhondda — sitting magisterially on the sideboard, mantelpiece, on a shelf of the dresser or on top of the piano were the family's ancestors. Not literally of course, but in sepia photographs in carved and polished wooden frames, ornamental brass or decorated china ones. Sometimes they hung on the wall, as in Tydraw, single hand-tinted portraits. Whatever, once inside the house, in parlour or back-kitchen, despite the friendliness and warmth of the welcome, there they were, staring down at you with disapproving eyes. At least they looked disapproving, as nobody ever smiled in these photographs, not even the babies and children. Solemnity and misery were the order of the day for the young, while the adults exuded a mixture of boredom, patient resignation, bad temper and occasionally arrogance.

On reflection this was not surprising, considering how uncomfortable they must have been. Young girls stood erect in best black bombazine long-skirted dresses with frills and tucks on the close-fitting bodice. Their feet were forced into tiny, shiny, fitting ankle-boots with rows of buttons to do up and their hair was tightly drawn back from the face into a bow at the nape of the neck. Mothers usually sat in the one chair, hands piously crossed on their lap, unless they had an over-dressed baby to hold, while the husband stood proprietorially behind or to the side, one hand on the back of his wife's chair and the other napoleonically in his jacket or bent awkwardly behind his back as though caught in a half-nelson. Now and then I came across a photo where the husband sat and the wife stood, clearly indicating who was the boss in that household. Children either stood dismally around or sat on stools next to the upstanding father. When the stools discreetly merged with the background or were hidden by long skirts, young girls towered above their dad looking like junior giraffes.

These backgrounds puzzled me for a long time, too. The photograph of the Thomases's ancestors, two doors up from us, showed them in a room with Corinthean pillars and velvet drapes. I was surprised at this, as the Thomases were ordinary people who lived in a humble terraced house like us. Evidently their forefathers were grand people who had lived in a mansion somewhere. Further confusion ensued when I asked Mrs Thomas (Lizzie Ann) where this was and she replied: "No, they didn' live in no mansion, gul. 'Alfway up second street they lived."

On our piano there was a photograph of my father when a boy of about ten with his parents and two sisters. They all looked very disconsolate as though not even a chocolate marshmallow would bring them a measure of joy. My father's hair was plastered down from a centre parting on his head, which emerged from a stiff white Cromwellian collar. At the other end, knee-length, ample breeches, long, dark stockings and highly polished mid-calf boots completed apparent discomfort. There they all were, sitting and standing around at the end of a path leading from a beautiful rose garden. Now I knew they had lived in our house. But our back garden was nothing like that. Apart from the odd yellow flowering weed, the only plant we had was mint, which did, it is true, produce a pale violet flower after it had rampaged and gone to seed. I couldn't believe any house on the Tump had a back garden like that, so they couldn't have borrowed someone else's for the photo. Perhaps they had gone out, bought a lot of roses and stuck them on poles in the garden and on the bakehouse wall. It seemed unlikely, though.

There was a girl, Maureen Jenkins, older than me, who lived four houses away and when my mate, David, wasn't around and she had nothing better to do she would condescend to be my friend. One of her forebears, a most formidable looking matriarch, glared down from her back kitchen wall onto the table where the family ate. I always felt uncomfortable in the presence of this fierce-faced lady, so when given a biscuit by Mrs Jenkins preferred to eat it in the scullery, garden or even sitting on the front door-step, away from the evil eye. One day I asked who this person was.

"Oh, that's my mother," said Mrs Jenkins. "She was a lovely person, the soul of kindness. Never without a smile on her face. A truly good Welsh woman. Friendly and hospitable like all Rhondda people."

Looking at the savage-faced old girl stuck up on the wall, I found this hard to believe. However, I came to the conclusion that ancestors' photos served a double purpose, the most important being that their censuring gaze made their descendants think twice before doing anything they shouldn't. Perhaps we should have more of them around today.

Coming from a not very gadget-minded background, my parents had no camera — not that these new-fangled things were exactly readily available during the war years. Of course, the progress of the youngest member of the family had to be regularly charted, and had been since I was a few months old, as there were photos of me lying and sitting on cushions. I only really became aware of these trips to the photographer in Mill Street, Pontypridd, when I was at the more discerning age of four, and I hated them. But I did discover the secret of the beautiful gardens and mansions.

Mam would pack into a carrier bag my carefully ironed best frilly dress with a pair of silk shoes and sometimes a big hat made of gauze and ribbons. After changing in a room at the photographer's, I would be stood on a box in front of the garden, mansion or woodland scene with waterfall, with my mother fussing around arranging my hair under the hat, fiddling with my dress, puffing up the sleeves, pulling up my socks and sometimes, to my embarrassment, my knickers. When finally she was satisfied, for some unfathomable reason I was given a basket of imitation flowers to hold.

"Now, Mary, stand very still and give a nice smile. The gentleman won't take long."

Sometimes there would be an unexpected problem. I might cough or sneeze, drop the basket and scatter the flowers, dislodge my curls and unpuff my sleeves. Then the arranging performance would be repeated. Sometimes when the photographer was nearly ready under his blackout and I had been warned to watch out for the dicky-bird — which I never saw in a dozen visits — an urgent desire to pee would overcome me. "Mam, I want to go to the toilet."

"No, not now, Mary. The gentleman's ready."

"But I've got to, Mam."

"Try to hang on, Mary. There's other people waiting to have their photo taken."

"I can't!"

"You must!"

If I snivelled, looked as if I was going to cry or started to writhe and cross my legs, I would be hurriedly bundled to the toilet. After all, a photo of a little girl in her best dress with a basket of flowers would be spoiled with a puddle at her feet.

The photos always turned out to my mother's satisfaction, though I didn't like them much.

One year the photographer's only free appointment was on a Saturday afternoon when my father usually took me out somewhere and my mother looked after the shop. If Pontypridd RFC had a home fixture in Ynysangharad Park we would sometimes go to watch them play. It was raining this particular Saturday afternoon and as my father was taking me I already had on my frilly dress under my coat, and leggings covering my white socks to keep them clean. It was decided there would be no gauze picture-hat on this occasion, so all my father had to do after removing my outer clothes and rainhat was to comb my hair and wipe the wet from my shoes.

On arrival at the photographer's, Dad was shown the box to stand me on. Without further ado and to my surprise he lifted me up. Perhaps his mind had been elsewhere when my mother was giving her instructions.

"Daddy..."

"Yes, love?"

"Aren't you going to take off my coat and comb my hair?"

"No, love, you look all right like that."

His mind evidently hadn't absorbed Mam's instructions. Far be it from me however to change this much more satisfactory state of affairs, so I said no more, but just stood watching for the elusive dicky-bird.

A week later, Dad and I collected the photos from Mill Street. "There you are, look. Lovely photos. Your mother will be pleased with these." I wasn't so sure.

Back home, my mother's expectant smile turned to an expression of shock on taking the photos from the envelope, as she saw my happy figure, wet hair stuck to forehead under lop-sided rainhat, scarf tied in muffler fashion, leggings sagging over muddy shoes and hands in big woollen gloves clutching a little damp handbag. "Oooh, what's this? Oh, Jack, look at these photos. You didn't even take her wet rainhat off. Nor her coat. And she's got her pretty lemon silk frock on underneath. And look at the shoes!"

"Oh, never mind, Sal. She'll have to have more taken. I think they're nice, anyway. It's the first photo she's had, she's smiling in."

"I dunno. If I don't do everything myself..." Mam went on.

Unfortunately Dad was never deputed to take me to the photographer's again.

CHAPTER EIGHT
Christmas
and the Bakehouse

Most of the tales about his youth and stories about his working life and courtship of my mother were told me by my father in what was generally regarded by all and sundry as his den or retreat, the bakehouse. This was built above the cellar, and its outside wall was on Bryn Eirw Hill. It was reached by climbing up the steps from the back yard to the small garden, and its normally open door when my father was ensconced within welcomed you after two more leg-stretching steps up to the right.

It was a male kingdom to which my father repaired when he had a spare moment or when he wasn't in a good mood. When he was in a bad mood, he went down the Vaughan's Arms or to bed, frequently to both in that order. I was never allowed in the bakehouse on my own as it was too dangerous, with different kinds of saw — hack, tenon, crosscut, fret — lying around on trestles or boxes, and the huge, paint and glue-splashed wooden work-bench which occupied half the space was littered with nails and screws of all shapes and sizes, hammers, chisels, screw-drivers, planes, mallets, drills, awls, adzes and vices. The latter were attached to the bench and had long metal handles which could whizz round in either direction to open or close the gleaming steel jaws as required. There were drawers and boxes containing tin-tacks, gauges, bits, markers, set-squares, spirit levels, folding wooden rules with brass hinges, strange flat pencils, mitre boxes and steel measures curled up in circular metal containers, which after being pulled out would fly back into their little round houses when a small central button was depressed. On one shelf were woodworking and carpentry books, manuals and magazines.

Dad was forever warning me about the terrible injuries I could incur through careless movement. With an intake of breath and opening his eyes so that the whites could be seen all the way round, he would say: "Oh, for goodness' sake don't go near that saw; I've just sharpened and set it, and if you dislodge it, it could take your arm off, mind," or: "Keep away from those chisels, for God's sake; they've got edges like razors and could go right through you." These alarming exhortations worked, as the only mishap I ever suffered, and that frequently, to my mother's annoyance, was to bespatter my clothes with paint, or oil spilt from a sweet little round metal can with a long thin spout.

My father would tell horrid tales of bloody, often fatal accidents with tools at the test-beds, especially circular saws:

"Oh, nasty accident at work today, Sal. One of the carpenters, in a hurry, see, didn't use the guard on the circular saw... Tut! Cut his arm through to the bone. Rushed to the East Glam, he was. He'll lose the use of that arm. Blood everywhere."

And he would tuck into his sparerib and mashed swede with relish.

Another gory story concerned his own Stanley sprung screwdriver which he kept in his trug in work. Two men, one a relatively new employee, who plainly didn't get on, kept arguing during the day. Finally the new man, losing his temper and seeing the maroon wooden handle of my father's screw-driver in the trug nearby, grabbed it and approached his adversary.

"This bloke went right up to Dai Amos, pressed the button and the screw-driver shot out right into his stomach below the ribs. He's a madman, mun. Could have killed him. Might have, for all we know. Anyway, Dai was rushed to the East Glam and the police took this mad fellow away. Deserves all he gets. Would be my accursed screw-driver, of course."

My mother would look suitably horrified, hand to mouth, teeth on lower lip and would say as a natural feminist ante-dating the movement: "Oh, his poor wife!"

Wood shavings littered the bakehouse floor, and should a screw or nail be dropped, it was lost forever. But it didn't matter, as my father had thousands, and the place, quite unlike anywhere else in the

82

house, was a delightful, glorious but organised mess, as Dad could always put his hand immediately on whatever he wanted.

The bakehouse ovens had last been used to bake bread in my grandmother's heyday. Another door in the end wall, directly opposite the door to the garden, allowed easy access for flour and yeast deliveries, avoiding their having to be carried through the house and, when the loaves were ready, for easy distribution by cart around Trehafod.

When quite small I remember the ovens being stoked up at Christmas time and people from the Tump queuing up at the bakehouse door with pale Christmas cake mixture in rectangular baking tins. The iron door of the oven would grind open on its massive hinges and the cake tins were put on a wide, flat, spade-type contraption with a detachable handle and pushed deep into the hot blackness, to emerge some hours later, risen and transformed into a rich, brown, delicious-looking cake containing currants, nuts, cherries, dried fruit and not without a fair dash of alcohol.

These doors set opposite each other also caused a mighty draught to rush through the bakehouse in winter, freezing one's lower limbs, but this was combated to some extent by a paraffin heater which gave out more glow and smell than heat. This served to melt little cauldrons of glue and shellac, which looked like the trays of toffee lumps in the shop that needed breaking up with a small hammer.

When I was quite small, my father made me a wooden swing with slatted sides and a back which he slung up on hooks embedded in the open roof rafters. Seated on a soft cushion placed between the bars, legs dangling but above the draught, and sucking a lollipop, I would swing back and fore in the shadowy half light cast by the storm lamp and the glow of the paraffin heater and watch him as he smooth-planed some wood or made pretty dove-tailed joints on corners, and listen to the tales he had to tell about his life as a boy. I frequently awoke in my small bed in daylight and felt a surge of disappointment not to see the shadows playing on the brick walls and smell the scent of wood and glue and baking, because though the oven was cold, a charcoal smell still permeated the atmosphere.

When I was in Hafod school, the swing gave way to a canvas bag such as sailors carried, which was stuffed full of shavings and rags. This was hung on the ropes which had previously held the swing and dangled lengthways down to my knees. It was a punch-bag. Seeing me arrive home from school tearful on occasions and with a swollen lip, scratched face, bruised cheek or bloodied nose, Dad had decided to teach me not only to defend myself but also to give as good as I got if not better.

"If they know you'll fight back and hit them hard, they'll leave you alone," my parents said. So Dad attempted to teach me to defend myself.

"What a waste," I thought, "to learn all this boring boxing business, pummelling some silly sack and hurting your hands, just to land one punch on some bully's nose!"

But Dad obviously knew what he was talking about because it worked. Shortly afterwards, the school scram-cat, Agnes Edwards, came at me during play-time, claws out on the end of flailing arms, and got her come-uppance.

"Straight to the nose, mind, no swinging your arm," my father had coached. "And remember, lead with your left, defend with your right."

However, I was a southpaw, having a reluctant left arm which had been broken when only three years old at the elbow when I tried to fly. My left arm didn't like leading and in the heat of the moment I had no idea which was left or right, north or south. My face had been previously and painfully disfigured by Agnes's nails, so on her wild, snarling approach, one fist pushed the thrashing talons aside while the right connected straight with a small, upturned, button nose, which suddenly changed from pink to bright red — streaming red. Howling and screaming: "She've broke my face, that Mary Davies 'ave broke my face!" she was led off by her acolytes, somewhat diminished in number by her downfall, while my friends, some newly acquired since the punch, hedged their bets.

"Cor, see that? That showed her, the old scram-cat! Spect you'll have the cane for fighting now, Mary," they almost gloated.

Which I did. But at least it didn't show like scratches on my face.

The punch-bag, having outlived its usefulness, was dismantled and my father built a lathe where it had been, in that part of the bakehouse not occupied by work-bench. This was a fine piece of apparatus, composed of planks of wood, iron wheels, bands of thick strap material and a wooden pedal which when pressed rotated the wheels and the object to be turned. Neighbours came to admire the lathe and my father's cleverness in making it. It almost opened up a new career for him, as candlesticks, bowls, vases and ornaments of every imaginable guise poured forth from its revolutions to meet the demand for wooden pieces, especially at Christmas. This was also a boon for my mother, as whenever a customer or one of their sons or daughters got married, they were given a wedding present, and now, instead of having to make a special present-buying expedition, or in the event of forgetfulness or a sudden wedding, having to choose one of the unused market gadgets, wedding gifts were close at hand, offering a wide choice, free (to a certain extent) and of better quality.

Newly established Trehafod homes could hardly deem themselves properly set up without one of my father's turned wooden articles. Usually the wood such as pine was lightly varnished, and mahogany darkly, but sometimes he would chance upon a piece of beech, elm or oak with a beautiful grain and, incorporating the grain in the shape, would turn it carefully, use the finest sandpaper to smooth it and, handling it as gently as he might unstable gelignite, wax it until the beauty of the wood emerged and it became more a work of art to be savoured, caressed and smelled than a useful household item.

Everything was of course not always sweetness and light in our home. Despite being a normally happy little family, we were like any other in that the occasional upset occurred, although my mother was one of the persons least prone to extended fury and grudge I ever met. She would get angry, shout, and that was the end of it. Two of her favourite maxims were: "Peace is better than gold" and "Don't let the sun go down on your anger". My father was a hard worker. It was second nature to him whether he liked it or not, and he was more readily affected by the stresses and strains of life. Unlike my placid, even-tempered mother, he was easily upset and sometimes it was she or I who would unwittingly be the cause of the upset. A wrong look, word, decision or accidental criticism, and if the time was ripe, he would be off.

"Oh, I've had enough of this," he would say. "I'm going north!"

After many years of annually hearing this statement, I could smile at it, but when I was a youngster it created great dismay in my heart. Where was north? Aberdare? North Wales? Or Scotland? Was he just going there for a quick visit to get over his bad temper or for a longer holiday or, worst, leaving us for good? And what would we do for money and someone to protect us from burglars and drunken men? I had heard of rugby players 'going north' to play a different sort of game, but my father was too old for that and anyway didn't play rugby.

In the event he went south, not north, down Bryn Eirw to the Vaughan's Arms, where, he would announce, he was going to have "a skinful", and after an hour or so come home and, without speaking to anyone, go straight upstairs to bed, or up the steps to the bakehouse where he would hammer nails.

My mother didn't seem unduly disturbed by this performance but the atmosphere in the house was not as relaxed as normal. Mam had no relief other than me to serve in the shop, and I was often not much use, not knowing all the prices and being too small to reach half the things. She would say: "Oh, your father's in one of his paddies again. Hm! Men! Still, I suppose they all have them."

I dreaded the approach of meals at such times, as my mother would prepare my father a tempting tray.

"Take this up to your father, Mary, there's a good girl."

I would knock on the bedroom or bakehouse door to warn my father of my arrival, and on seeing the tray he would growl: "Take it away. I don't want it." If I tried to plead with him to eat it, so he would be less likely to go north where he wouldn't have such tasty food, he reiterated: "Take it away, I said. I don't want it. If you don't take it, I'll shot it down the stairs, mind." So, when little, I would hurriedly remove it from his irate gaze and struggle back downstairs with it to prevent further upset. He only used this strange phrase when in this frame of mind and I would reappear in the kitchen, breathless, arms aching with the weight of the tray, tea slopping all over it, and report to my mother that he had threatened to shot it down the stairs (or the steps, if he was in the bakehouse).

In later years, still being despatched with the tray, I couldn't help smiling to myself at his predictable words and would say: "Okay then, that's up to you. But it seems a bit childish to me, and you'll only have to buy more cups and plates and clean up the mess." And I would leave the tray. After a while reason would tickle its target. The food would eventually be eaten and finally he would reappear, looking sheepish, and the 'paddy' would be over.

When I was older still, if I arrived home to find my father not in his usual place, pottering around in the house, shop or bakehouse, and sensed an atmosphere, my question to Mam: "Oh, Dad's gone north again, has he?" would evoke a wry smile, and, like naughty little girls, we would have a giggle at the ways of men.

Particularly during the war years, Christmas seemed a bigger festival in importance, preparation and enjoyment than since and although everything — food, toys, cards, trees — was in short supply, people's spirits were high as the celebrations compensated in a small way for the deprivation and sadness of the rest of the year. No sooner was one Christmas over than the next was being looked forward to and prepared for.

Although there was a general shortage of toys for Christmas, this was not the case as far as Tump children were concerned, because in December the shop was not so much 'Philly's' or 'Jack's' as 'the Toy Shop'. During the second half of the year, my father spent increasing amounts of time in the bakehouse with his *Manual of Toy-Making* on the bench with his pieces of wood, glue and paint. Gradually the less cluttered area near the oven would be enlivened with scooters made of wood, including the wheels, painted with whatever colour paint was available; battleships — these always painted in grey with one thick black and two thin white diagonal stripes down their sides — with little bits of dowelling for guns and a mast; chunky, khaki-green camouflaged tanks; shiny, black armoured cars; and grey aeroplanes with red, white and blue circles on their wings. For younger children there were clowns, parrots or rabbits which, with a piece of wood like a pencil stuck through their bodies, would balance and roll over and over along parallel bars; and monkeys on trapezes which flung out disjointed arms and legs as they jumped and somersaulted when manipulated by squeezing two wooden shafts.

One favourite, an ingenious toy, had four or five wooden chickens on a table-tennis bat, linked by cord through small holes in the bat with a weight underneath. When the bat and consequently the weight was rotated the chickens would noisily peck imaginary food on the bat's surface. The faster the bat was rotated, the harder and faster the poor chickens' beaks would hit the surface, so that one week after Christmas most were beakless and many headless as well. Children loved these and parents tolerated the noise because it was

Christmas, and longed for mid-January when they would be simply table-tennis bats and life more peaceful.

Cricket bats were simple to make, so in war-time cricket replaced football as the winter game, and for years after the war was over the Tump couldn't field a successful football team, but they were local champions at cricket.

There were rocking-horses, dolls' houses, prams, cradles and chairs, rifles and guns, skipping ropes, push-and-pull animals on wheels, carts with coloured bricks and railway engines and trucks. When ack-ack-ack or eeeeh-eeeeh-eeeeh sounds were heard around the village, it was nearly always one of father's guns or planes held aloft by a boy being a British soldier or pilot, shooting down Germans.

So during December the shop, although bare of good things to eat, had a cheerful air about it, with the colourful toys spread out for display on the shelves and in the window. Requests such as: "A pound of flour, two candles, a Milky Lunch and two ounces of Welsh mints" were replaced by: "Two lorries, one rocking-horse, a monkey on a stick and two warships, please".

One year, overestimating youngsters' enthusiasm for the Navy, Dad, with my help in painting the side flashes, made too many battleships, and about a hundred of these still lay around in the bakehouse in January. Although being brought up on a farm, my mother was not slow in adapting to a more commercial world and proved a good business woman. When on her bi-weekly shopping outing to Pontypridd, armed with a sample ship, she intended to approach a few war-starved stores which in normal times stocked toys to offer to sell them the warships. The first, Leslie's Stores, gladly and unhesitatingly accepted, and my mother left with a cheque and a promise on her part not to approach any other shop. They even went so far as to send a van to fetch the ships and displayed an interest in buying any other spare toys. It seemed no sooner was the idea born than the plan was executed and Leslie's main window on Taff Street was piled high with little grey battleships with black and white side flashes. My pride knew no bounds, and to my mother's embarrassment I stood on the opposite pavement, pointing to the window and proclaiming to the passers-by: "My daddy made those and I painted the black stripes!"

Although Christmas was well past, the ships did not last long in the store and some joy was brought to the hearts of potential British sailor boys further afield.

In those days a chicken dinner was a rarity unless you happened to breed them and had bought chicks early on in the war, so sausages, chops, liver or rissoles were frequently consumed for Christmas dinner. My parents had attempted breeding hens but they caused considerable problems — the proper nourishing grain for them was generally unavailable, they wouldn't lay, and they kept escaping over the wire fence, hiding in outside lavatories and pecking at neighbours' carefully grown vegetables. They caused chaos in the back gardens, because our own garden was too small for them to strut around freely and they destroyed the herbs, which were the only plants we ever grew. It was such trouble keeping them, we usually killed them after a few months and ate chicken dinners on consecutive Sundays in mid-year. They were skinny, scrawny birds anyway and not fit for a Christmas feast.

Every Christmas, Tydraw provided us with a well-fed, tender young chicken, bred in situ and far more successfully than our back garden fowl. For some reason the Tydraw bird was always presented to us live and we could choose which one we fancied for our dinner. First it needed catching and my father would resignedly undertake and finally make the capture after first having an undignified chase around Cae Bach, once causing the unfortunate bird to take refuge down the well and almost drown. Once seized, the squawking, indignant creature was bundled into a sack, which was quickly tied up. Whatever the weather it was necessary to walk back to Trehafod over the mountain as my father couldn't very well take a thrashing, protesting, monster chicken in a sack slung over his shoulder onto the bus. Once home, it was allowed to roam in the cellar until evening, the eve of Christmas Eve.

Then, when all was quiet, when the sounds of socialisers returning from the Vaughan's Arms had faded and bedroom lights in neighbouring houses had been put out, my farmer's-daughter mother, well practised in the art, would quickly and neatly put paid to the chicken with a sharp knife by finding a special nerve in the roof of its mouth and, with a quick stab, puncturing its brain. The blood would be allowed to drip down the drain in the back yard. My feelings were in turmoil: pity for the chicken but admiration for my mother. Even if cast on a desert island, as long as she was there, we would survive.

"My father was the expert at this," Mam would say. "When he killed a chicken, you hardly had to pluck it. The feathers would fall off."

Apart from the initial cacophony when taken from the cellar, it didn't utter a sound. Later the poor thing, with its limp neck hanging to one side, was brought into the kitchen for plucking, which was most easily done when the body was warm, and more easily still if the killing had been carried out properly and the special nerve found. Then methylated spirit was poured onto an enamel tartplate, set alight and the naked chicken moved over the flame to burn off the hairs.

By the time the chicken had been stuffed and trussed, I had stopped feeling sorry for it and was eagerly looking forward to its succulent slices on my plate. I would pray for its soul in church in the morning. My mother always sent my father and me to the eight o'clock communion. She was of the Annibynwyr persuasion, so didn't have to go to church.

Cooking dinners, especially the more comprehensive Christmas kind, was a feat that had to be seen to be believed in our house. True to our mining environment, it was almost entirely done with the aid of coal and one small gas ring. My father got up early to rake out the ashes of the previous day's fire and build a new masterpiece, sticks for which had been drying since the previous evening in the oven which was part of the range. So eager to enflame was the carefully constructed pile of fuel — tinder-dry wood, crumpled up pieces of newspaper and various sized pieces of coal — it never took more than one match. Baden Powell would have elevated my father to a Scout peerage had he known of his fire-building prowess. By the time my mother was up, the fire would be roaring in the grate, licking its lips in anticipation of cooking the pans of potatoes, sprouts, parsnips and tinned garden peas, and the oven would be heating up like billy-ho for the chicken.

As the morning wore on, the pans simmered or bubbled away, near or on the fire, each taking its turn to repose on the red coals or have its chance on the gas fire to speed on the cooking process. Occasionally water boiled over onto the flames, which then made a dreadful fuss, hissing and spitting and steaming so that Peter would back away uncertainly from his place on the mat and seek a surer refuge under the table, his anxious brown eyes peeping out from time to time. Meanwhile the face of the cook was gradually going puce in the intense heat. The moment when the cooking of the bird was completed was fraught with anxiety. As the shop was open until mid-day for the people to collect their Christmas orders, a customer would come ostensibly to help manoeuvre it out of the oven but in reality to have a glass or three of elderberry, parsnip or rhubarb wine. In fact there was a constant stream of customers coming into the house on Christmas morning to sample the home-made wines, or at least what was left of them after several bottles had, as always, popped their corks with a loud explosion, not unfamiliar in those war days, and sprayed the wall-paper with delightful-smelling but distasteful-looking purple or yellow stains. My father started with communion wine early on Christmas Day and, steadily topping up with home-made during the morning, drinking the health of practically all his customers, he presented a beaming face and expansive disposition to his Christmas dinner, then spent the afternoon sleeping it off, the only day in the year when he took to his bed (apart from the annual 'paddy').

Uttering ooohs and aaahs as fingers and hands accidentally brushed hot metal and spots of grease spat on bare arms or face, we manhandled the big bird in its sea of fat in the big roasting dish out of the oven and onto the table, Mam holding one end, Dad the other, me hovering one side and the customer opposite.

"Careful!"

"Up that end a bit, the fat's spilling! Ouch!"

"Oh, it's cooked lovely. I hope it's nice and tender, Jack, not like that old, tough thing of ours we had in the autumn."

By the time it was sitting on its throne we were all puce in the face.

Residents of Trehafod didn't seem deprived during those war years. People managed to get a few things together, even if they had for several months been making, or buying, if lucky, and storing. War Christmases certainly didn't sound as bad as those when my father was a boy, as all the presents he had in his stocking, so he said, were a few nuts, apples and oranges. He had known one poor lad who had had lumps of coke placed in a stocking he had hopefully hung up — for being so presumptuous as to expect anything at all!

My mother was a dab hand at present making. Every year she would make a rug to go in front of the fire for us (or rather for Peter, as he monopolised it) and for Tydraw. Each evening from early autumn she and I would have the partly made rug over our knees and, in cosy, intimate mood, get to work on it, chatting, me about school and her about the old days, or listening to *Just William*, *Dick Barton*, *Special Agent*, *ITMA*, *Monday Night At Eight*, *The Carroll Levis Show* or *In Town Tonight* ("Once More We Stop the Mighty Roar of London's Traffic...") on the wireless.

The rug was made by cutting up material into identically sized strips — my job —- which my mother would insert with a sharpened, one-legged peg into a large square made from a sack, or perhaps two sewn together, with an old but tough blanket or a dismembered coat as a backing.

No unwanted garment was ever thrown away and Mam made pretty patterns with the different coloured fabric strips. She also made bed-covers out of squares of different cloth sewn together, and eiderdowns if she could get her hands on lumpy stuffing material called kapok.

She knitted socks on four needles — the most difficult and complicated operation I ever saw — and when she was turning the heel, I wasn't even allowed to speak, so total her concentration needed to be.

"Mam, Mam, look, Mam, by there. There's a..."

"Ssh, Mary, shhh for a minute while I do this blooming heel. Now, six there, five there, three..."

Glasses slipping to the end of her nose, tongue curled over her lip, her attention to the job was absolute. A few minutes later: "Right! Now then. What did you say? Oh, that's a difficult old bit just there, that is."

"Well, what I was saying was, a black pat crawled from under the chair onto your shoe and disappeared. I think it went up your leg."

And so Christmas would pass for another year and on Twelfth Night we would put away the home-made cards, hand-made, glued and painted paper chains ('trimmings' as we called them) and the ordinary light-bulbs covered in poster paint of different colours to enliven the scene in the shop window, until we could once more take them out in twelve months' time and greet each other with the compliments of the season.

CHAPTER NINE
St Barnabas' Church

I was born on a Sunday at six p.m., welcomed into the world by the bells calling the parishioners to Evensong in St Barnabas' Church, one of the oldest unconsecrated church buildings in the lower Rhondda, opened in 1892 when it was in the parish of Llantrisant. As parish boundaries changed, it later belonged to Llanwonno and in 1914 finally and permanently settled down in the parish of Llanddewi Rhondda. It was on the other side of the road, opposite our house. As soon as I could walk I was made to answer the call of those bells, sent to practically every service by my mother, who, as she frequently reminded us, didn't have to go herself as she was of the Annibynwyr faith and her chapel in Castellau was too far away to attend. She determined to bring up her daughter as a good, Christian, church-going girl.

My father was luckier than me, only sent at Christmas, Easter, Whitsun, the Patronal festival in June and sometimes Harvest, and when his duty was done at the eight o'clock communion he could have the rest of the day off. In effect I went unprotestingly across the road as church enlivened an otherwise dull and uneventful day, and really I suppose it was the social highlight of the week on the Tump, for when else could a girl wear her best coat, hat and shoes?

The church services, especially Evensong, were an excuse for the Tump's own fashion parades. If anyone had new clothes, out they would come on a Sunday evening, and be shown off as their elegant owners walked slowly to church, chatting in small groups or standing around outside the porch when the service was over. Some people were positively unrecognisable in their Sunday best. Women became ladies and men, gentlemen. The women, normally in pinnies, flat lace-up shoes, thick brown lisle stockings and hair tortured in curlers, appeared as chic models in colour-coordinated outfits, fitting coats with full skirts and fur collars, matching hats with pretty feathers jauntily piercing the air and shoes with heels high enough to prettily arch the instep. Hair in training for curls all week long was released in all its glory for Evensong on Sunday. The years dropped off these ladies and went on holiday for a few hours, to return the following day with the household chores. Hearts were uplifted with the weekly beautification and the hymns and psalms would ring out joyously so that those non-church-attenders, or those regulars having an evening off, were convinced they were missing something and wished they had made the effort and gone after all.

The Trehafod gentlemen were similarly transformed. Mine workers, so black that only the whites of their eyes distinguished them from the lumps of coal they hewed, factory workers in sagging navy dungarees, caretakers in brown twill coats with pencils stuck in breast pockets, bus drivers in creased, smoke-smelling uniforms, all were metamorphosed on Sunday evening and elevated to the upper classes in appearance.

Smart charcoal-grey or navy pin-striped suits were lifted from hangers, carefully ironed and folded white shirts with starched collars and sober ties, restrained with a gold pin, were donned and, smelling of moth-balls, the men walked down the street stiffly in order not to wrinkle the razor-sharp crease in their trousers. Brylcreemed hair shone under the lamplight or in the sun. There was much chat, joking and laughter, especially after the solemn service, and people wouldn't rush home to catch the latest episode of the classic serial on the radio before the nine o'clock news. I frequently felt annoyed that I lived only six strides from church and hadn't the opportunity to peacock-parade home like my friends and the ladies and gentlemen. I always caught the classic.

The upstairs windows of all the houses opposite the church and within eyeshot were net-curtained, and for the entry and exit of the fashion parade the housewife residents would hover unseen and peruse the new fashions, commenting on them the day after in the shop.

"Oh, Ceridwen's got a lovely new saxe-blue suit. She looked very smart in it last night going to church. I can't understand she's not married."

"In church again last night, was she? Well, she 'aven't missed a Sunday for ages. If you ask me, she's after the curate."

"I wasn't too keen on Betty Lloyd's 'at, were you? That's new, too. Well, I haven't seen it before, anyway. It looked as if it 'ad a load of grass 'anging off one side!"

"No, green feathers, they were, gul. Very fashionable. And she's always wearing that ol' fur coat, in' she? Duw, duw, she must get 'ot. Whatever the weather, winter or summer, she've got that fur coat on."

"Aye. And she might as well stop wearing it now, 'cos we all know she's got one."

Barnabas was a fairly unpretentious saint, not quite managing to be one of the Big Twelve, and although he was a good mate of Paul and had a few adventures with him, they also had their disagreements. Barnabas had a farm which he sold, donating the money to the poor in Jerusalem, living up to his name which meant 'Son of Encouragement' — and an encouragement his church certainly was to those of the Church in Wales persuasion in Trehafod.

St Barnabas's Church in Bryn Eirw is, like its patron, also unpretentious. It stands exposed and open to the weather at the junction of Church Hill and Bryn Eirw Hill, protecting the terraced houses opposite and a little clutch of three or four cottages adjacent to it and lying gratefully in its shadow. In this it recalls the great mediaeval cathedrals of Europe, guarding the dwellings of citizens clustered in refuge far below their lofty spires. But the Trehafod scene is very much a modest, miniature version. St Barnabas' has no spire, no tower, no stained glass in its windows, and only one small bell. No splendid site entered by lych-gate and surrounded by graveyard with yew trees adorns it; there is indeed no graveyard, the church not being licensed for marriages, funerals or burials. The vestry wall looks onto the street like the houses opposite it serves, but there is a narrow strip of healthy weed and flourishing thistle-invaded grass on three sides. A little courtyard outside the entrance porch overlooks some steps which take you to a path leading to a mysterious, rarely disturbed door at the back of and underneath the church. I suppose it was a store room for things like the tea-urn, trestle tables and spare chairs that were needed for special occasions.

1. Author when father took her to be

2. Author when mother took her to be

4. Jack, 1935

3. (above) Paternal grandparents and children Anne,
   Rachel and Jack (aged 10)

5. St. Barnabas' Church and shop
   (with open door, opposite) from
   Kemp's Pond, Llwyncelyn, 1960

6. Sal (c. 1935)

7. Painting of Tydraw from road below Ton Hywel. Smilog, Bristol Channel and Somerset in distance. Painted by E. Wheeler, 1979

8. Tydraw – kitchen entrance and bailey, late 1940s

9. Tydraw - steps up to loft, late 1940s

10. Standard 4. Hafod School, 1946. Miss E. Roderick on left. Miss Lally Davies, headmistress, right. Author, second row from back, fourth from left

11. (above) Trehafod children.
St. Barnabas' Church and
top of Bryn Eirw Hill looking
to lower Trehafod with bridge
over river, 1965.

12. Lewis Merthyr colliery winding gear

13. Upper Trehafod (the Tump)

14. Infants Sunday School class,
    (c. 1953), Mrs Thyer on left

15. Lewis Merthyr Colliery
    in the 1960s

16. The river Rhondda flowing
    past Lewis Merthyr Bridge

17. The author, aged 8

St. Barnabas' Church

T R E H A F O D

JUBILEE SOUVENIR

JUBILEE SUNDAY - MARCH 8th, 1942

SERVICES:

8.30 a.m.   HOLY COMMUNION

11 a.m.   MATINS AND SERMON

2.30 p.m.   CHILDREN'S SERVICE

Preacher at 11 a.m. and 2.30 p.m:—
Rev. WILFRED LEWIS, B.A. (Vicar of Pentyrch)
(A former Curate of this Church)

6 p.m.   EVENSONG AND SERMON

Preacher: The Rev. Canon HUGH WILLIAMS, M.A.
(Rural Dean and Vicar of Llanwonno)

Unlike most churches, the interior gives an impression of light and airiness owing to the absence of stained glass and stone pillar and arch. The one central aisle in the nave, because subsidence affects the lie of the land, leads down to the altar which has never witnessed marriage, confirmation or funeral, although many would have had it otherwise. St Barnabas' has heard the cries of countless babies echoing round its walls, starting the faithful off with christening, but cannot help them on their way or see them off.

It is more reminiscent of the Welsh valley chapel than the traditional church, except for the absence of a gallery, as it is small, light and friendly. The polished, light-brown pews are movable, unlike the massive seats in dark, grey, stone-walled, awesome churches, which look as though they are wedded to the floor after centuries of sitting. Indeed, the pews were sometimes removed to one side to make way for the annual Sale of Work stalls and the occasional children's party, the vestry alongside being too small to accommodate these.

The little organ needed pumping manually and produced a wheeze which gave an extra dimension to the music in that it encouraged the congregation to sing out to drown the noise. You knew the people were in fine voice and the collection would be a good one when the wheeze was only heard at the dying away of the "Amen" ending the hymn or the "As it was in the beginning is now and ever shall be, world without end" for the psalm.

The male choir, a few regular tenors and basses and an everchanging gaggle of little boys — in the choir for a promise of reliability rather than a singing ability — slid almost unnoticed from the vestry into their choir stalls around the side of the organ. Occasionally, and this was rare, if the verger was indisposed one of the gaggle would be press-ganged into being the organ-pumper for the service. Once, although Miss Celia Downing, the organist, was playing furiously away for the hymn after the sermon, no musical notes issued forth. The congregation waited, then sang unaccompanied. The cherubic, exhausted, hot and bored choirboy, attired in cassock and surplice, had fallen asleep on his stool in the darker corner between the organ and the vestry door, blissfully unaware that his services were urgently required.

There was a ladies' choir opposite the men's on the other side of the aisle, contraltos at the back, sopranos in the middle and girls at the front. If a good-looking boy joined the choir, the numbers of girls interested in a singing career quadrupled and the following week the poor boy would spend the entire service red-faced and sweating, with eyes cast down, ogled by several admiring young females. He would either be gone the next week or brazen it out and become one of the peacock-strutters with slicked-back hair and not unobtrusive tie. I believe the women's choir was there not so much to sing as to keep the gaggle in order. Facial expressions were numerous and nearly always disapproving on the ladies as they frowned at a boy picking his nose or stared, eyebrow raised, at another as he whispered to his neighbour, jabbed him in the ribs with his psalm-book or ate sweets from Philly's bought with money intended for the offertory.

St Barnabas' was primitively and unevenly heated by hissing gas fires placed at intervals high up on the walls. If you chanced to sit underneath one of these, you would soon be generating enough body heat to boil up water for a cup of tea, but in mid-church you would freeze. The choicest seats in cold weather were of course in between. It was possible to turn off but not turn down these appliances by pulling a clanking chain hanging beneath. It was either all or nothing. However, first, the clanking chain attracted every gaze with its noise, disturbing the service, and secondly, being in church and of necessity concerned with matters of loving one's neighbour and putting their welfare before your own, you could hardly deprive them of a bit of warmth. Living so close to the church, I tended to dash in just before the final bell finished tolling and the only places left were the hot seats. I never actually fainted, but my hair curled. To this day I attribute waves on either side of my head above my ears to the church services when, as I grew taller, one side or the other was scorched and frizzed by the gas heaters, for nowhere else does my hair curl.

The church was cleaned every week by a family of worshippers called Hole, and with their cumbersome aluminium buckets, scrubbing brushes, dusters, polish and brooms, Mrs Hole and her daughters did an excellent job. There were no vacuum cleaners or other electrical devices. In fact I think there was no power supply to the church for the task was done with cold water, fetched and carried across from our house. Personally I wondered why the church needed such thorough cleaning, as people all bathed on Saturday night and went in their best clothes on Sunday. No litter was thrown about, the choir boys and girls carefully putting their sweet papers in their pockets to avoid leaving evidence of misdemeanour, and only rarely were jam sandwiches smuggled in to be nibbled during the sermon.

However all was spick and span and the pews highly polished. If you were early and found an empty pew, you could slide in at one end and your momentum would carry you in a sitting position ten feet further on to the other end of the pew by the wall. This was a great attraction in Sunday school before the superintendent, Jacob Maddocks, arrived. As children weren't allowed to play ball games, hopscotch, hide and seek or any other game in the street on a Sunday, they went in their hordes early to Sunday school to indulge in this illicit pastime. The verger, Emlyn, was about, in his greying black robe, but his admonishment: "Hey! Stop it! I'll tell Mr Maddocks about you, mind!" was ineffective and unheeded. Part of the fun, I'm sorry to say, was harassing Emlyn, who must have hated Sunday school, and getting him to chase you round the pew, faded black gown flying. Some bold, irreligious boys of God-fearing parents, who had part of their collection money left after buying sweets in our shop, used the rest of it betting on the bum-slides.

Sometimes during the service people would nod off, heads drop forward, and the occasional snore be heard, making the offender jump and sit up straight, eyes blinking and sliding guiltily around to see if he had been noticed. On one occasion a short, chubby, friendly woman, who walked up from lower Trehafod near the school, fell asleep in her seat. She made no snoring noises but on the polished pew began to slide forward, then stop and sink lower until only the crown of her hat was visible. The congregation behind her watched and held their breath and the vicar in the pulpit also seemed to be anxiously looking in her direction more than normal. There was no one near to bestir her without interrupting the sermon, so people just prayed she would wake up or hold firm. However, God must have been indulging his sense of humour because the prayers were unanswered. A sudden last slip, the hat disappeared from sight and with a loud bump the lady landed on the floor. Startled, everyone in front of her turned round but there was nothing to be seen. Emlyn, sitting at the rear in one of the big, fixed, separated seats, was immediately on his feet to help but poor

Miss Jellings was already on her way up, fingers clutching the back of the seat in front, hat askew on her head and glasses awry on her nose. There was no damage done, only to her pride, and the vicar carried on preaching.

Church was not normally a hilarious affair, especially on the dark winter morning when, being sent to early communion, I discovered that the congregation consisted of myself and Emlyn. The curate was there of course, and besides mixed feelings of panic and hopes for postponement I felt relieved that at least it wasn't sung eucharist, which would have meant a weak duet, at least on the female side. The service did go ahead with much mumbling on my part and greater concentration than usual on standing and sitting as there were no examples to follow. I did get a much bigger drink of the Blood of Christ than I normally did and although the collection that service was only sixpence, the curate gave me two squares of chocolate on my way out and said he'd be over for a cup of tea in five minutes. Sometimes he had breakfast as well after the early communion.

Throughout the church's history there can have been no more faithful a servant than Emlyn Rowe, the verger, from Top Street. He must have held that position for thirty years or more, yet the number of times he missed a service could be counted on ten fingers. When he was away the whole village knew within an hour as it was prime news. How could the church manage without him?

"Ol' Emlyn wasn't in church this morning. Got a bad cold apparently."

"Never! How'd they manage?"

"Oh, not very well. One of the sidesmen took the collection but the bell-ringing was awful. Too early, and it didn't go quiet, like, at the end like Emlyn does it. Funny without him there."

"Oh, yes, not the same at all. If he was bad for long, they'd miss 'im, mind."

He was generally known as Old Emlyn though he was ageless. Despite having what I thought was a baby face, albeit with dark jowls, he had looked seventy all his life. He was small and moved with a forward-leaning shuffle, rarely looking to right or left. Always pleasant and courteous, he was shy, with a nervous laugh, and a man of few words who didn't like to look directly at you. He was unmarried and lived with his sisters. He was to be seen daily

100

returning from work about five o'clock but without his black verger's robe with velvet shoulders he was scarcely recognisable.

"Oh, 'ullo, Emlyn. Didn't notice you for a minute. How are you today? Lovely day."

"Hmmhmmhmm. 'Ullo. Orright thanks. How are you? Yes, lovely day. Orright then. So long."

And nodding his head he would shuffle off up Bryn Eirw hill, not really wanting to chat but most anxious not to give offence by showing it.

Being the verger he took the offertory plate around during the penultimate hymn. Church regulars were sent booklets of little, dated packets to put collection money in and we had three of these, kept in the book-case with the prayer books. There was one for my father, who used his four or five times a year, one for me, the attender-in-chief, and one for my mother, who never went, because she was Annibynwyr, but whom they clearly hoped to see in church or they wouldn't have kept sending her a booklet of packets. Practically all these little envelopes found their way back to church via me. In fact the money we gave was returned to us after each service, as unfailingly every Sunday Emlyn would trot across to the shop once or twice with bagfuls of change, the coins having been depacketed. One of my parents would give him a bank-note or larger value coins for them, always making up the collection to the nearest round sum. I did suggest to my mother that there was really no need for me to go to church so much because we could always give Emlyn the collection when he brought his change, but she would have none of it.

At some services such as the midwinter eight o'clock communion the offertory wasn't worth bothering about, but for others, particularly the harvest festival with visiting vicar, the church would be so packed people would be squashed up like peas in a pod in the pews and extra chairs were put out to line the aisle. Then three or four sidesmen were needed to help collect the offertory because Emlyn would never have got around during the hymn on his own. Sometimes, if he had 'the rheumatics' and was slow shuffling around, or people dropped their money on the floor or couldn't find it in their pocket, the last verse had to be sung a few times to see the offertory procession through.

At the shop after the service and seeing a beaming Emlyn holding a bulging bag: "Oh, good collection tonight then, Emlyn. How much have you got there?"

"Hmmhmmhmm! Yes, good one tonight, Mrs Davies: Five pounds eighteen and sevenpence ha'penny."

"Oh, church packed out was it?" (She knew it was as she'd spied in the strategically placed mirror upstairs, conveniently positioned near the window.)

"Hmmhmmhmm! Yes. Had to put out more chairs in the aisle, mun. Lovely service. Good preacher, that chap from St Luke's, aye."

"Right you are then, Emlyn. Here's six pound."

"Oh, thank you, Mrs Davies. Hmmhmmhmm! Right then. Tara, Mrs Davies. So long then. See you next week."

Harvest was undoubtedly *the* service of the year. On the Saturday the Mesdames Hole did an extra cleaning before the behatted ladies of the choir arrived to decorate the church, bringing flowers, fruit and vegetables of all kinds, and to receive contributions from the Sunday school children and the village people. Cauliflowers flanked by cabbages, parsnips and onions were stood on window-sills and carrots, cucumbers and tomatoes guarded the font. Thoroughly washed, humble potatoes filled in spare spaces and the pulpit edge above the ladies' choir was lined with apples, pears and oranges. These were later changed to lettuces, gibbons and radishes after a particularly large jaffa rolled off during one of the harvest services, perpetrating a mini-avalanche, and landed on a choir-lady's head, knocking her hat off, to the choir-boys' hilarity, and nearly knocking her out. Oranges and bruised, split apples rolled over the floor and squashed pears were on people's best coats, some even sat on by those short-sighted ladies carried away by the hymn and unaware of what was happening.

The altar was the *chef-d'oeuvre*. Always, apart from during Lent, beautifully and artistically arranged with flowers, it now also had besides fruit and vegetables two big sheaves of corn made out of delicious-looking bread baked a golden brown, with realistic stalks, ears and plaited binding. Works of art indeed! Between these always stood a big lump of shiny coal to remind everyone that without this commodity it would be difficult to pay for the rest and that we were giving thanks for what lay beneath the earth as well as above it.

As well as a visiting vicar there was a harvest procession, with the brass cross from near the lectern at its head carried by an older reliable choir boy. No slipping in around the side of the organ for the choir at harvest! As the organ pump wheezed and Miss Downing began to play the processional hymn, the gleaming cross appeared at the main door, followed by the smallest choristers, necks and ears thoroughly washed for the occasion, increasing in size to the men and finally the visiting vicar at the rear. Few eyes were on hymn-books though the hymn was sung lustily, as most gazed at the slightly embarrassed procession, and it was a thrilling experience to hear the treble and soprano voices, then the louder tenors, strong baritones and booming basses in turn as they passed by close to you. Harvest hymns must be the most tuneful and lung-bursting sung during the year. They do not quite have the familiarity of Christmas carols but as the organ intones, the heart and mind are uplifted at the recognition and pleasure of meeting an old friend only welcomed once a year. The harvest service was like a good play — you were sorry when it was over.

On the Monday the produce was distributed to the local needy and hospitals and the delicious looking sheaves were cut into chunks and slices and given to the parishioners. It was virtually uneatable, dry, hard and crumbly, as bread in those days had no preservatives, so my mother didn't really know what to do with it. It was usually left on the mantelpiece as a kind of paper-weight for letters until it shrivelled up into a horrid, curled-up lump and was thrown out with the ashes.

Afternoon Sunday school was if anything better attended than the adult services, especially as summer approached, because regular small worshippers were given a free ticket for the annual June outing to Barry Island. Jacob Maddocks, caretaker of Trehafod's Memorial Hall, which comprised a library, smoking and billiard rooms and a concert and dance hall with a stage, was the only church-goer brave enough to take on the job of superintendent, and suitably stern he looked in his Sunday garb. A short, stout, balding man with glasses, he could, despite twinkling blue eyes, give quite severe disapproving glances when wearing his stiff white Sunday collar, which often appeared to be throttling him as his face became redder as the afternoon progressed. Having to come from lower Trehafod, with Sant's and Bryn Eirw Hills to climb, he arrived a little later than most of the children and until his whistle was blown to start proceedings, chaos reigned. Children chased each other around the church, up the pulpit, slipping under the pews and sliding along them. Boys played shove-ha'penny with their collection money and wrestled and jumped on each other in the aisle. Babies bawled and were slapped by their sisters, girls admired each others' frocks and sometimes came to blows in arguments over the prettiest, others sucked sweets or lollies and chocolate dribbled from mouths down chins and onto best coat, shirt and jumper fronts. Amongst all this a monitor would be conscientiously giving out hymn-books, calmly stepping over bodies locked in combat on the floor, ducking to avoid the occasional kneeler flying through the air or the hymn-book just distributed, as though totally unaware of the tumult and mayhem all about. Emlyn would be wringing his hands in the middle of all this, uttering: "Hey, you! Stop it!" and: "Oy! You mustn't do that!", not knowing which naughty boy to pursue or screaming baby to placate, there were so many, trying to grab a body as it hurtled past, finally rolling his eyes hopelessly before quitting the scene, vanquished, and leaving the barbarians to get on with it. Miss Downing's face would peer around the organ from the vestry and hastily withdraw in horror at the sight before her, which might have been the inspiration for Hieronymus Bosch's vision of Inferno.

Then a shrill whistle blast would be heard and chaos became order in a split second as panting children regained their seats and sat stiffly, holding their breath and with only their eyes moving. Superintendent Maddocks had arrived! Miss Downing would decorously emerge to play a well-known children's hymn which would be enthusiastically and untunefully shouted rather than sung by the assembled battalions. Then the under-fives would solemnly file out, wide- and innocent-eyed, hand-in-hand, to the vestry to be entertained and taught by Mrs Thyer for half an hour.

My mother always referred to this lady as 'poor Mrs Thyer' because she had incredibly bad eyesight and even with the thickest possible lenses in her glasses still saw only with difficulty and would hurry past her husband, the local barber, when he came to meet her after church. As she also walked at a fair lick, despite her infirmity, he was often to be seen apparently chasing her through the Trehafod streets but in fact merely trying to catch her up to escort her home. She was marvellous with the small children, who reciprocated her affection and came in crowds to the Sunday school. Their large numbers were the reason her class was hived off in the vestry where they sat in rows on low benches and where there was more room for their action songs. She told or rather acted Biblical stories for them and the little faces, mouths open in wonderment, would follow her every movement and utter 'Ooohs' and 'Aaahs' with a sharp intake of breath. After a brief rest came the action songs, and they would sing these on their way home as well as in church, little hands and arms making shapes and waving up and down as appropriate with facial expressions to match:

> The foolish man built his house upon the sand (repeated)
> *with heads to one side, and shaken sadly to denote foolishness*
> The rain came down
> *waggling fingers in a descending motion to represent rain*
>   and the floods came up
> *lifting motion with hands in upward scooping motion*
> And it all came tumbling down
> *shaking heads and bending over to touch the floor with their hands*

The second verse was an altogether happier affair, accompanied by smiles:

> The wise man built his house upon the rock (repeated)
> *looking happy and nodding, and building a house shape with hands*
> The rain came down and the floods came up
> And there it firmly stood
> *with fingers pointing triumphantly.*

One song which thrilled them, as it could be made personal to them, went as follows:

> When the sunshine's over -----

here you put the name of your town/village/hamlet or if the name was unsuitable you could simply put 'My village' or 'My valley', but 'Trehafod' fitted perfectly, so the children eagerly sang:

> When the sunshine's over Trehafod
> My whole world is bright and gay
> For we all like living in Trehafod
> And God soothes our cares away

105

Sometimes the songs had only a tenuous Biblical alliance but all taught the little ones about life and gave them an early introduction to simple philosophy and sensible thinking.

CHAPTER 10

Outings

lthough as a family, including Auntie Rach, we went for a week's summer holiday most years to resorts such as Porth-cawl, Llanstephan, Ilfracombe and once a long way to Pwllheli in North Wales, the best outings were the day ones spent with friends of the same age. These were sometimes to local places of interest, organised by Hafod school, or sometimes a street trip, or the annual church trips, one to Barry Island and one local picnic-cum-sports excursion.

No tickets were required for the latter. Anyone could join in, as you walked to the appointed destination. If the weather was bad, it was simply postponed to the following Saturday and large, hand-written notices were placed in our shop window and on the wooden board outside the church normally used for election information:

THE ST BARNABAS CHURCH OUTING TO TYLAWINDER
DINGLE, WHICH WAS POSTPONED BECAUSE OF
INCLEMENT WEATHER, WILL NOW TAKE PLACE SAT.
NEXT, AUG 3RD.
SANDWICH MAKERS PLEASE MEET IN THE VESTRY AT
9.00 AM AND VOLUNTEERS TO CARRY PICNIC ITEMS AT
9.30. THANKYOU.

SIGNED: THE CURATE.

The postponement notice was more terse:

ST BARNABAS CHURCH
JULY 27TH.
PICNIC OFF — RAIN.

CURATE

107

— as the Reverend Corbett had to speedily write half a dozen sheets for display around Trehafod and deliver them himself.

Parishioners set off at various times during the morning, those with impatiently cavorting youngsters early, the ladies of the choir and the spinsters later. Some spoilsports would be scathing: "Hmmmph! I'm not walking all that way for a cup of tea and a pink salmon sandwich, thank you very much. I'll stay 'ome and 'ave a bit of peace!"

Families who lived next door to each other walked together, and all took their own extra supplies of sandwiches, cake and pop. After the initial brief, upward haul to Sherry's Pond, just above Top Street, the children were already demanding nourishment and a rest, so barely ten minutes after leaving home the food was unpacked and a good portion devoured. The steep mountain path then lay ahead, going up to the left. Halfway up the mountain it turned sharply right, still ascending steeply until the midway point was gratefully reached, where the ground was level for a hundred yards or so, giving the walker a breather before the final trek to the top, again going left. Most people, having conquered the first, steepest, stoniest slope, took a rest, sat down to admire the magnificent view and regirded their loins for the remaining climb.

Admiring the view was an excuse for an extended rest at this point. To one's left could be seen the interlocking spurs of the narrow Rhondda Valley, fading into the blue-haze distance, settlements strung out in the valley bottom and perched on the hillsides. Immediately below was the silver ribbon of the river, lazily snaking through the village. On the main road the few cars looked like black pats slowly moving forward, and people resembled ants as they walked on the pavements or worked in the colliery, in gardens and allotments or played in the park. A toy train, a white smoke trail billowing from its engine, puffed up the track under the rust-coloured rock of the lower part of the valley wall and the waterfall on the Llwyncelyn road looked like a motionless white sheet hung out to air.

On our way over the mountain on a visit to Tydraw, my mother, out of breath at this point, would always say: "Oh, we'll have a little spell here, Mary." I liked these little spells as they always meant a sweet to suck as well as a stop, though we never sat down. Gelliwion mountain, apart from the well-trodden path, was covered in fern,

108

moss and bracken, and in spring dead, brown ferns abounded, leaving little space for the new, tender green shoots to grow. My uncles' sheep and lambs wandered all over the mountain, sometimes standing uncomprehendingly to watch mountaineers and at other times bleating pathetically and ambling awkwardly away after heaving themselves heavily to their feet on their stick legs.

At the top of the mountain my mother would say: "Oh, look at all those ol' dead ferns, stopping the little lambs getting to the new shoots. I know, we'll burn them off. But don't tell anybody, will you?" and she would take a box of matches out of her pocket and set fire to the mountain. We'd carry on to the farm and every time she would tell me how my grandfather Richards used to burn off the old bracken to allow the sheep to get to the new grass.

On the way back we would see a small, charred spot where the fire had burnt. Once however the flames had extended over a huge area and one section was still smouldering. My mother was rather dismayed to see this. "Oh, dear, I didn't expect it to spread so far," she said. We could see the blackened patch clearly from our kitchen window and evidently most of the population of Trehafod had watched the raging flames, as we soon discovered. Next day in the shop my mother was horrified to hear one of the customers say: "Hmmmph! Vandals been setting fire to the mountain again. Did you see those massive flames yesterday, Mrs Davies?"

"No, gul. We were out all day yesterday," she answered quietly.

"I dunno. People can't leave things alone, can they? I don' know what the world is coming to."

"Yes, it's awful isn' it?" Mam said without conviction. Having turned a charming shade of pink, and seeing me trying to suppress a grin, she made a face at me when the customer wasn't looking and put a finger to her lips, quickly shaking her head to tell me not to give the game away.

Just off the summit road is a level path to a watering spot known as Jacob's Well. Pure, sweet-tasting, ice-cold water gushed from a rock slab at this point and tumbled down the mountain as a shallow stream to be dispersed in a boggy patch a little lower down where myriads of wild flowers grew profusely. Hikers brought receptacles to carry home the water, said to have certain beneficial properties. Courting couples often made for Jacob's Well, as it was a grassy area enclosed by thick ferns where they could bill and coo undisturbed, and people were content to stop there for a refreshing drink. It was a productive area for whinberries, and walkers with empty tins searched around in the grass for hours collecting these delicious, elusive wild berries.

Approximately a quarter of the church picnickers got no further than Jacob's Well. Hot and sweating fathers, carrying the smallest sons or daughters on their shoulders up the steep slope and hauling another by the hand, would be glad to hear their equally purple-faced mother or mother-in-law announce that enough was enough and they weren't going any further for fear of dying of heat and exhaustion.

"Oh, let's have a sit down, for God's sake. You lot can go on if you like, but I'm stopping here. You can pick me up on your way back. I got no more puff left in me, see."

Some made it to Jacob's Well, some to the mountain summit, but only the hardiest to Tylawinder, so the St Barnabas faithful, in various states of prostration, were scattered over the mountain like Uncle Dick's sheep. Those who reached the dingle were rewarded with a few warm salmon sandwiches, seed and fruit cake, and hot tea made from water in kettles lugged from Trehafod and boiled over a twig fire. Clods of earth were built into dams to create little pools for children to splash about in. The curate, Mr Corbett, organised games and the choirmaster, Mr Haydn Lloyd, some community singing to finish off. Then it was time for the long but easier trek homeward, sunburned faces glowing, fern-scratched legs stinging and eyes squinting into the sun low in the western sky over Coedcae tip.

Since such a large number of the church members never arrived at the picnic venue, the following year it was decided not to go quite so far and for not quite so long. Just beyond the top of the mountain, amongst the ferns, was a strange, rectangular piece of grassy land the size of a football field, ideal for sports, which would take place in the afternoon. People were exhorted to make a serious effort to get there and not give up en route.

"Try to avoid having a sit down on the way up the mountain," said the curate. "That's fatal. If you sit down you'll probably fall asleep after your exertions or stay there for the rest of the day."

And trying to encourage the stiff, the lazy and the overweight, he cited the example of Gwyn the Milk, no spring chicken, who made the journey every day. So, flagging enthusiasm for church picnics somewhat renewed by Mr Corbett's encouragement, and because he was much liked anyway, people made the effort and hordes could once more be seen trudging up the steep paths. Kettles and the salmon sandwiches, seed and fruit cake courtesy of the choir ladies were again transported to the mountain top and halfway up some of the men collected water from Jacob's Well in jugs and bottles for the tea.

The walk was no problem for my mother and me as we weekly made the trip to Tydraw either over the top or under the Western tip, going up past the bungalows and 'the Vaughanies' — a pleasant enough family who had built a shack to live in on the mountain side and who were consequently regarded as gypsies. My father of course had to stay home to mind the shop though there was no need as few people remained on the Tump. "Oh, I'm not too keen on these bunfights, Sal. You and Mary go. I'll look after the shop and have tea ready when you come home."

Perhaps holding sports competitions following a stiff climb wasn't such a great idea after all. Children had tried to settle the sprints by having races against each other up the side of the mountain and were too tired to give of their best. Others, showing off their athletic prowess, had run all the way up and promptly dropped with exhaustion at the top. Someone forgot the measuring tape for the jumps, the ball for the longest ball-throw got lost in the ferns when the boys used it for football, there were a few crocked ankles on the uneven ground in the three-legged race and only two sacks could be found for the sack race, so there were about fifty heats and five finals. Children grumbled that the high jump wasn't fair as it was judged by proportionate leg length to height jumped, so the winner was a small girl who jumped level with the curate's knees while a tall girl had gone over a height level with his waist! Mr Corbett organised everything with his usual energetic enthusiasm and cheeriness and everyone enjoyed their food, even if the troop arriving back in the village resembled a bunch of war veterans.

There was a suggestion by one of the choir ladies, seconded by nearly everyone: "Curate, next year, why don't we have the picnic and sports on the football field?" This was in mid-Trehafod, the far side of the river. "Save us that ol' march up the mountain. An' if we forget anything, someone can easy nip back to the church for it." One wag concluded: "Nah, mun, 'e'd rather take us to the top of the mountain, 'cos we're nearer to God up there!"

Undoubtedly the excursion of the year was the Sunday school outing to Barry Island in mid-June which was eagerly awaited and talked about for months. New faces appeared in Sunday school every week for some time beforehand, the bedlam increased and it was the worst time of the year for Emlyn. Tickets and instructions were given out the Sunday before the trip, the only Sunday in the year when threats induced good behaviour, and afterwards children returned straight home concentrating on not losing their precious little bit of cardboard. Tickets for accompanying adults were sold in the vestry on the Friday evening and parents were pestered all week by their offspring not to forget. As if they could! The Tump had been expectantly agog for at least a fortnight, hoping for fine weather, listening to weather forecasts and making or buying new clothes to wear. Mountains of sandwiches were prepared, the shop was emptied of pop and biscuits and on Saturday morning there was, at least an hour before departure time, a steady stream of assorted families making their way to the station, the little ones clutching buckets and spades, fathers in open-necked shirts guarding the bag of food and mothers in colourful frocks carrying the bathing suits and towels. The scene was similar if it was drizzling, but bright clothes were concealed by light macs and umbrellas were held uncertainly aloft, their owners peering hopefully at the sky.

The stationmaster-cum-guard-cum-porter. Mr Emlyn Jones, of little Hafod station was much in evidence as he punched holes in tickets, exhorted people to stand back from the platform edge, ran off to get more toilet paper for the ever-lengthening queue at the lavatory, and attended to the flag-waving, shutting doors and whistle-blowing for the ordinary trains entering and leaving the station, which were greeted with cheers by the assembled trippers, especially those on the down line.

Much excitement attended the boarding of the Barry Island Special, usually shared with one of the Trehafod chapels, Bethel, Bethesda or Penuel. No sooner had people settled in their seats and even before Pontypridd station was reached, children were asking: "Are we nearly there?" and when told "No", after a pause they would anounce, "I'm 'ungry, Mam". Mam would answer: "No, you're not." After a few exchanges, Dad would sigh, get up and reach for the food bag above in the luggage net. The proffered sandwich would not be consumed so much as spread over the compartment, egg on the floor, crusts on seats and crumbs everywhere as the child squirmed between people to look at the sepia photographs of distant, exotic resorts around Wales: Tenby, Llandrindod Wells, Aberystwyth. Excitement diminished, children sitting on laps gazed out of windows at the passing scene while bold boys stuck their heads out and got grit from the engine in their eyes, or leaned out dangerously to wave to a mate in another compartment. Fortunately the GWR did not supply corridor trains on the valley lines or the ructions would have been worse than in Sunday school.

Over-excited children who had fallen asleep were woken up when the coast was in sight and that first glimpse of the sea was perhaps the best moment of the whole trip. Necks craned, people stood on seats and each other's toes to see, depending on the weather, the glittering or gloomy stretch of grey water into which soon white bodies would shiveringly venture.

Deck chairs were hired and taken onto the beach when fine and people struggled, scratched their heads and fell about laughing at their inexpertise in setting them up. Whoever invented the transatlantic liner deck chair had a wicked sense of humour. The plumper ladies then usually found that, once sunken into the depths of the deck chair, they had great difficulty getting up without much hauling, pushing and more merriment, so stayed there all day, newspapers over their heads and, with stockings and shoes removed, revealed deathly white, blue-veined legs which would be sun-burned bright pink and somewhat sore at home-time.

If the day was drizzly or threatened rain, the trippers crowded their deck chairs in the two shelters, one at the peaceful eastern end of the promenade near Nell's Point and the other at the western end where all the children begged to go but were never taken. Near this shelter were the shops selling beach goods, toys, rude souvenirs, jewellery, sweets, rock and candy-floss, the ubiquitous 'tray for the beach' and chips, chips, chips — because, as Gwyn Thomas said, Barry Island is the kingdom of the chip.

Whatever the weather, once the family was settled at a certain spot and recognisable markers as to position had been established, kids would impatiently peel off the remaining clothes they had been gradually discarding since getting off the train as they marched excitedly to the beach. Some already had their bathing costume on under their clothes, others, wrapped in slipping towels, wriggled into theirs, putting them on inside out and back to front. But who cared? The sea was awaiting them, usually on the horizon, and all they wanted was to race to its inviting but cold embrace. The tide was invariably going out as people arrived and as the rise and fall of the water in the Bristol Channel is one of the highest in the world it was often a long way away. The race became a walk, became a sit down, as kids gave up the chase and played with the water left in the hard, rippled sand, or turned across to the rock pools and the concrete, sea-water swimming-pool. They inevitably got lost and some were always taken to the lost children's office, where their names were loud-speakered over the beach. However, anxious parents would always cough up for an extra ice-cream or candy-floss on recovering their children, so some canny little exploiters got lost and found on purpose.

Some didn't mind being apparently abandoned so long as they could carry on digging their way down to the Antipodes.

"Look at that little *dwt*," my mother would say. "Fair do's. She's been digging away for hours, all on her own, kokum as anything. Here you are, go and give her a sweet, Mary, poor little dab. Wonder someone don't come looking for her!"

I didn't mind at all the weather being dull or cold, as around dinner-time my father would say: "Too cold for sandwiches today, Sal. Come on. Let's go and get something hot to eat." The neighbours would look after the deck chairs, the bags, the towels and the assorted belongings, and we, me hopping with excited anticipation, would go off to Forte's restaurant and have fat chips and ham and to follow a scrumptious, entrancing-looking peach melba or ice-cream sundae. It set your mouth watering thinking of it and was more beautiful to look at than all the pictures in all the galleries in all the world. Arranged in a tall, elegant glass, the three obtainable flavours of ice cream, vanilla, strawberry and chocolate had flaky chocolate and chocolate sauce swirled around them and fruit of various kinds. You found bits of nuts and jam sponge in this delicious mixture, which was topped with real cream and two crisp, triangular wafers either side of a moist maraschino cherry. The lot was consumed with a long-handled spoon, only seen in cafés, and for me was the treat of the day.

Between the railway station and the beach, some enterprising gentlemen by the name of Collins had set up a fun-fair, renowned throughout South Wales, so it was impossible to set off on the homeward journey without passing this irresistible attraction. If the train's departure was at six o'clock. people would pack up on the beach at five o'clock and placate their nagging children by passing an expensive hour in the fair. Children saved their pocket-money for various rides months beforehand, and altogether families spent enough money in that one hour to keep themselves fed for a week.

"Oh, never mind what it costs. What I say is, it's only once a year, isn't it? And you got to enjoy yourselves and have a bit of fun now and then, gul, 'aven' you?" was heard on all sides.

My parents had little to fear from my demands in this respect, as once, on the annual holiday, I had travelled on the water-chute in the Coney Beach fair in Porthcawl — a simple operation, going up a steep incline in a little open carriage and coming down its neighbour at speed, to pass through some water at the bottom before rounding a tight corner to come to a sudden, bone-jarring halt. My stomach had been left some hundred feet higher up, but stomach or not, on completion of the exercise I was violently sick. I was a fair coward, to my shame and annoyance. I didn't mind watching others being turned upside down and whizzed round and hurled through the air, but didn't want to undergo the experience myself. I had to admit even to being afraid of a trip on the prancing horses on the merry-go-round. About all I could manage was a Round the World Cruise, provided my father had his arm firmly encompassing me. The Ghost Train was definitely out, but once I bravely ventured on the Dodgems, beseeching the driver to keep to the outside and avoid the other cars and, hanging on for dear life, didn't open my eyes until the ordeal was all over. I quite liked the Penny Falls and the All-Win Deluxe machines in the amusement arcades, where a little metal ball sped around and ended up in one of a little row of cups, eight winning ones and two losing ones, one at either end. Nine times out of ten the ball headed for the end cups and I scoffed at the machine's lying name.

Friends would ask, going home on the train: "Cor! Did you go on the Octopus? Whew, it was great, aye." Another would boast:

"I went on the Scenic Railway four times. Aw, it was smashing. Everybody was screaming their 'eads off!" I'd have to reply that, No, I didn't go on these things (both horrid, stomach-churning rides) as we'd left the beach late, or I'd lost my bathers, or some such excuse, secretly wishing that I could like and be brave enough to participate in an experience that everyone but me appeared to enjoy so much.

Jaunty hats bearing the messages: EVERYONE LOVES A SAILOR and DON'T PINCH ME, KISS ME were in abundant evidence on the train home, as were fluffy pink elephants and china dogs, won through skill or luck on shooting ranges, coconut shies or dartboards. Children with red faces, cherubic mouths and spent limbs slept leaning against their fathers, sticks of lurid pink rock stuck out of bags and wet bathing suits peeped out of rolled-up towels. Sand was everywhere — in pockets, shoes, hair and on the compartment seats and floor. Whether the weather had been good or bad, people had enjoyed themselves and as they struggled up Church Hill, glowing pink due to sunburn as well as exertion, proclaiming they were parched and dying for a cup of tea, they looked forward to relating the day's exploits to a relative who had stayed home to look after the house and who would be awaiting their arrival with a pot of the much-longed for tea in exchange for a stick of rock with 'Barry Island' written all the way through it.

CHAPTER ELEVEN

The Lewis Merthyr

T rehafod grew up dependent upon but not actually around the Lewis Merthyr colliery which is situated on the northern edge of the village. Most of Trehafod extends south of it, hugging the main road and broadening out a bit where the valley widens in the direction of Hopkinstown and Pontypridd. Although I had little to do with the colliery, I lived close to it for eighteen years, taking for granted its sights and sounds. Miners, completely black but for the whites of their eyes and their pink lips, held no terrors for me as a child and I was never frightened by tales of bogeymen, although an evacuee friend from Finchley in London, Olive Hughes, ran and hid in the flood overflow pipe the first time she saw a blackened miner, and when the hooter blast was heard at the end of the afternoon shift, she would run home, saying it was time for tea although it was only three o'clock.

If men were practically unrecognisable in their Sunday outfits, they were completely unrecognisable in coal dust. I might be tamping a ball against the end wall of our house and a miner returning home would say: "'Ow be, Mary". To my uncertain reply he would continue: "Don't know me in my working clothes, do you?" and laughing at my shaking head say: "It's Olly Pugh, gul. I dunno, I was only in your 'ouse on Sunday morning, aye. And you don't know me now. Well, well. And I brought you some lovely beans for your dinner an' all." I was very sorry but, like sheep and Chinamen, unwashed miners all looked the same to me.

In later years pit-head baths were constructed, but by then the evacuees had returned to London with the notion that in Wales (pronounced 'Wells' or even 'Wews'), at a given signal, black

117

sub-humans crawled from holes in the earth and that signal was also notification for sensible children to hide.

The only times I found the mining fraternity eerie was early in the morning. Men would get up in the grey dawn light for the early shift and some individuals would take on the responsibility for wakening their work-mates or neighbours. This they did by knocking loudly on doors, a noise which resounded and echoed hollowly in the still, silent, dark streets. I could hear the knocking from my bedroom a street away and quieter at first, then loud and insistent on the door of a house immediately behind ours in Second Street. There were never any voices, only the knocking, then the metallic, rhythmic tread of hob-nailed boots on the hill next to our end wall.

I usually pulled the bed-clothes tighter around my chin, buried my head deeper in my pillow and tried to go back to sleep. But the knocking always brought to mind a story my father had told me about Rachmaninov's powerful *Piano Concerto in C Sharp Minor*. The composer had a terrible and illogical fear of being interred alive and in this piece he awakens to find himself prone in a dark restricted space — a coffin. Holding his breath and trying not to panic, he knocks loudly, hoping to be heard. The concerto starts slowly with three majestic chords and gradually builds up speed until there is a desperate urgency in the music as the composer realises what has happened to him, that he has been buried alive. Then the notes become more staccato, frenzied and clashing, as though someone is scrabbling and scratching on the coffin wall, probably tearing his nails trying to get out. Panic prevails for several bars; then the music begins to slow down and comes to a peaceful conclusion. Has he suffocated or been rescued? The end is specu-lation, depending on whether one's mood is pessimistic or optim-istic. Whatever, I associated this music with the miner — his lonely walk to what must have been a miserable job, entombed in the dark earth, never certain that he would emerge, and knocking on doors in a silent, early-morning world on his way, with only the stamp of his heavy boots for company. Rachmaninov must have had a Welsh soul even if a Russian name.

Apart from its topography, an extra hill above Trehafod, the Tump derived its name from the miners who spent hours squatting on their haunches, especially along what was called the New Road, a road directly connecting with Woodfield Terrace (Second Street)

118

and after a gentle descent linking with the main road to Porth. They resembled monkeys sitting on their haunches on an elevated spot or monkey-tump — hence the name, or so it was said. Their shift finished, and after a bath, meal and a quick glance at the newspaper, the *Western Mail, News Chronicle* or the *Daily Herald, Mirror* or *Worker,* and before going to attend to the care of their pigeons in the cote, miners would squat alongside each other and look out over their place of work, the football field and waterfall beyond, the Hafod Fawr hillside with the farms, green meadows and trees above, and the valley road stretching down over the river to lower Trehafod. They enjoyed the company of others but exchanged few comments or reflections, as they were a contemplative rather than a loquacious breed of men. Unsurprisingly, no sooner home and their needs attended to, they would be out of the house and squatting on their vantage point, enjoying the light and gratefully breathing the warm air after their incarceration.

Apart from this squatting position they adopted, you could always tell if a man's trade was that of a collier, as usually even when bathed they had black rings round their eyes and blue scars on their faces where a cut had healed without having been thoroughly cleaned.

Not counting the panorama from high on Gelliwion Mountain, along New Road was the best viewpoint on the Tump, and no doubt as a mother surveys her child's cradle the miners surveyed their colliery, where a special feeling of comradeship and belonging existed, like that among soldiers in times of war.

The Lewis Merthyr colliery was opened in the 1880s when the Hafod, Bertie and Trefor pits were sunk. It originated as the Coedcae colliery, but after being opened by Sir W.T. Lewis, chief administrator of the Bute estates and later Lord Merthyr, it was re-named. In August 1892 an explosion underground caused the deaths of fifty-eight men, but fortunately since then there have been no large-scale disasters.

Several of the Trehafod streets were named with the colliery association in mind. Two of them recall the philanthropic landowner, Lewis Morgan of Hafod Fawr. Wayne Street commemorates his nephew, Dr Wayne Morgan, who was also a churchwarden from 1893 to 1912 at St David's, Gyfeillion, built in 1853 on land donated by Lewis Morgan.

On hearing the hooters blare for the shift changes, I was always amazed at the vast numbers of men who poured in and out of the main colliery gates on Coedcae Road because the view of the colliery yard from the railings at the top of Church Hill was always one of calm and peace with few workers to be seen about the place. Large wagons in the marshalling yards stood idle, full of coal, or moved slowly forward and gently shunted the one in front, which carried on the lazy movement down the line with a light high-pitched clang as they touched and sometimes a squeaking of axles like the braying of a metallic donkey.

This was the end of the coal production process, the wagons being filled with clean, shiny coal and emerging from beneath the big, black, wooden slatted building on stilts and lining up for the transportation of Trehafod steam coal all over the world. These wagons used to join others coming down from the hundred or so collieries scattered throughout the Valley, the Lady Lewis in Ynyshir and the Pendyrus in Ferndale, to name two in the Rhondda Fach and the Parc and Dare, the Fernhill and the Tynewydd, remembered for its big disaster in 1877, four among many in the Rhondda Fawr, but by the late 1940s of which I write only three or four pits were still working. Throughout the mining period, millions of tons of Rhondda substrata were borne to the port specially constructed to ship coal at Barry, and to Cardiff, for export all over the globe. In 1910, the heyday of the mining industry, nearly ten million tons of the Rhondda passed through Trehafod on its way to Cardiff and Barry, which in that year between them handled nearly twenty-three million tons of South Welsh coal.

It was a sight taken for granted in the village, but a magnificent one none the less that would stop strangers in their tracks when, shortly after the hooter, the huge wheels with wire ropes leading down into the winding-house began to revolve in their gantries, standing proudly, black, greased and stark against the sky — the ultimate symbol of industry and man's taming of his environment.

If one has relatives or friends to visit in Llwyncelyn, slightly north of Trehafod and on the opposite, south-facing slope of the valley, the official route is a good two-mile walk by the time you have crossed the river, passed the British Legion Club and doubled back under the railway after Temple Buildings. Then, striking off towards the waterfall under Cwm George, with the few cottages of

Bridge Street on your right, you are on the Llwyncelyn road looking down on the swirling, fast-running river Rhondda and its rocky, convex bank and the football field next to it. The gaze rises to the colliery beyond, then up to the fine sight of the Tump. It is approximately another mile with a bit of an uphill pull at the end to Nythbrân Terrace, the first of the three Llwyncelyn streets.

However, if you took the unauthorised route across the colliery, using its access footbridge over the river, you could reach Llwyncelyn in ten minutes, or five if a colliery official shouted at you in vain to come back, then chased you off the premises. The main colliery gates were huge and fairly intimidating to children, but when they were shut there was a little in-built wooden door, normally unlocked, around which you could peer guiltily to assess the lie of the land before stepping through into the yard. Bold boys spoilt the chances of other trespassing youngsters who simply wanted to get quickly across the river to Llwyncelyn, because they went on to the colliery for adventure, to play and aggravate the duty watchman, who naturally developed an antipathy to children.

During the day, when the machinery was at full throttle, the colliery was a truly dangerous place even for the people working there, let alone the uninitiated, and the din was ear-splitting.

Fans at ground level would be blowing out the warm, used air from the pits, coal being sorted rattled deafeningly in the screens, the stacks would hiss and steam, and the sudden blare of the hooter made you start as would the clatter and unexpected arrival on the surface of a cage from deep down, carrying weary men covered in coal dust, blinking at the light and wearing their helmets with lamps attached to batteries worn on belts. The winding mechanism, meanwhile, added its grinding, churning, cog-engaging rumpus to all this and you'd have to be on the alert for trucks of coal bumping along the tram-lines crossing the yard, and above all for the Red Devil, which might appear, swerving rapidly around a corner, causing you to jump quickly aside or get mown down.

The Red Devil was not I think a typical piece of South Wales colliery equipment like the winding gear, the tall stack or the water-dripping washery, but was peculiar to the Lewis Merthyr. It was a motorised vehicle that looked like a slightly shortened, speedy milk float, painted red. Perhaps it conveyed urgently required machinery or tools from one part of the yard to another. It always

121

proceeded flat out, driven by a grinning fanatic bent over the steering wheel, who enjoyed seeing people taken by surprise and having to perform a standing lateral leap. More than anything in the colliery, even of the watchmen, I was wary of this Red Devil contraption and preferred to make my illicit crossing in the evening when the surface work was finished for the day. I would sometimes see the evil little machine parked near the clocking-on room, and even stationary it seemed to be watching you, ready to pounce if you didn't tiptoe past, avoiding accidentally disturbing the thing.

The clocking-on room was next to the lamp room, where hundreds of Davy lamps were lined up neatly on shelves and on the floor, counted out daily by the lamp man, and I always paused briefly to look in here and wave to Lew the Light, the night-duty lamp-man, a customer of the shop who bought ipecacuanha cough mixture for his bad chest.

Despite the noise during the day, there were never many workmen to be seen, and in the evening, apart from the man on night-watch duty, the only people you passed were those going the other way, from Llwyncelyn to Trehafod. Sometimes at the Llwyncelyn end of the covered footbridge miners would be going to or coming from the pit baths or canteens, but they never bothered anybody and wouldn't have cared if you held a Highland Fling in the place. It was strange to think that beneath you the earth was teeming with men manipulating coal-cutting machines, shot-firing, loading coal onto conveyor-belts and mine-cars, manning first-aid rooms and fire stations and shoring up tunnel roofs at the coal-face, because no matter what the time of day or night, a shift was working. In fact at night there was undoubtedly more activity beneath the Trehafod ground than above it.

On Friday afternoons it was not uncommon to see women waiting outside the main colliery gates when the hooter went for the end of the day shift at three o'clock, because Friday was pay-day.

Before the pit-head baths were built the miners emerged through the gates with black faces and dusty clothes, helmet with lamp having been exchanged for a 'Dai cap', but some still wearing leather knee-protection pads and carrying their tin tommy-box for food under one arm and a log for the fire under the other. Occasionally the food-box and a metal drink-flask would be suspended from their belt.

122

Hanging on a nail in the wall outside the kitchen door, every miner's house possessed a tin bath, either a long, thin bungalow-bath, rounded at one end and flat at the other, or a shorter, oval one with raised ridges in the bottom. Water was heated in buckets on the fire and as soon as one was emptied into the bath, another was put on to warm up. A great deal of the water ended up on the floor and the whole bathing business was quite a performance by the time the bath was fetched in, gallons of water heated in precariously balanced vessels, the miner washing with carbolic or coal-tar soap which now and then escaped and skidded over the floor, the final bucket being poured over the man's head by his wife to rinse him off, and finally the lugging out of the bathful of dirty water to the back yard to tip it down the drain. The pit-head baths, where men could shower in ten minutes, surely added months to a miner's life and a week to his leisure time in every year; it was one of the revolutionary inventions in coal-mining and must have been a marvellous inducement to recruitment.

When on Fridays the men hurried out, clutching square, beige packets, some were counting pound notes, others, taking out the change, were making their way to Cobner's shop for a packet of Woodbines and yet others would be hurrying the eighty yards down the road to the Vaughan's Arms, open until half-past three, to slake their thirst with a few well-earned pints of beer. A few would head for a very anonymous-looking building with a brown painted window — the betting shop in the little clutch of buildings at the bottom of Bryn Eirw Hill between Eileen's fish-shop and the undertaker's. I thought the men met by women always looked a bit embarrassed and faintly irritated. Were these poor wives with lots of under-nourished, skinny children, kept short of money by their husbands who would gamble away all their earnings? Were they men who drank so much beer that they would arrive home very late, unable to stand up, ready to beat their wives and offspring and with their pay packets empty, the result of temptation? They were probably neither — just wives on their way to town, Porth or Pontypridd, to do some shopping, and who had run out of house-keeping money, and the men hard-working, honest folk who enjoyed a fag and a pint.

Special double-decker buses waited outside the colliery at the shift's end before the era of the baths, as dirty miners covered in black dust could hardly travel on the service buses with their clean brethren. The scene resembled that outside the secondary school, with the buses lined up to transport girls to various parts of the Rhondda valleys. The younger children who were first out ran to be at the head of the queue and assured of a seat, then those too dignified to run walked at a fast pace and finally the older pupils and prefects strode out looking intellectual, bags under their arms.

On pay-days Mr Williams, the Trehafod policeman, and Jack Melen, the burly bobby from Llwyncelyn, were much in evidence on the scene and children did not dare to use the colliery as a short cut then. Although all Fridays were eagerly awaited, the most important one was in July at the start of 'Miner's Fortnight', when pay packets bulged with three weeks' money — wages for the previous week, plus two weeks' holiday pay.

Sadly, one of these occasions was the last day above ground for one of these local policemen. The heat, excited anticipation of the holidays, final preparations for settling down the colliery workings for two weeks and the general hustle and bustle was too much for Sergeant Melen, a tall, middle-aged, cheery ex-boxer, who suffered a heart attack and died on the yard. At the time my father was working there as a carpenter, and being a long-time friend of Jack Melen's was chatting to him when he complained of feeling ill, then collapsed. My father, desperately calling on his first-aid knowledge, was unsuccessful in trying to revive him and he died in his arms. It was a very upset, grim-faced father who returned from the colliery that day; the first time I ever saw him weep was when he recounted the experience. For some miserable hours it looked as though our holiday to Weston-super-Mare, due to start the next day, would have to be cancelled. I felt guilty at the time, feeling sorrier for myself who might not be going on the eagerly awaited holiday after all, than for poor Mr Melen. In the event we did depart as planned but Dad had to return for one day mid-week to go to the funeral and give details of the death to an enquiry. It wasn't too bad for him, however, as he had an extra return trip on the paddle-steamer from Cardiff docks.

The day after Miner's Fortnight began, the river was transformed from black, boiling, hostile, molten licorice with dust on its surface into a friendly stream, the bed of which, with its assortment of pebbles, stones and orange and grey pennant rocks, could be seen through the clear water. No fish appeared of course, even when it ran clean for several days, and there were no plants growing among the stones, just an assortment of rusty cans, bicycle tyres, discarded prams, broken wheels and old boxes. Now and then one espied a tied-up sack and suspected it contained the body of a cat or dog surplus to requirements. The river revealed all for two weeks in July, then the colliery washery resumed its work to clean the coal and the secrets of the water were hidden again until the following year.

The steeply sloping meadow below Hafod Fawr house, usually empty and uninteresting but for a few occasional geriatric grazing sheep, bluebell-picking children in spring and blackberry-gatherers in autumn, was suddenly brought to life by the appearance of the pit ponies. The little horses, normally stabled underground, were having their yearly holiday too and gambolled like lambs, rolled in the grass or raced the length of the field, manes and tails streaming. They nuzzled each other and played, tossing their heads, bucking and rearing, quite unused to the light, space and freedom. They were a great attraction to the locals, especially the younger element, who daily carried up food for them so that they returned to their jobs fat little animals with shining coats and sparkling eyes.

Meanwhile the mining population of South Wales descended on Porthcawl, staying in caravans in the Happy Valley and Trecco Bay camping sites, where they played on the beach, paddled, splashed and swam in the sea, romped in the dunes, laughed in the fair and in the evenings danced, sang, drank and strolled on the prom. Every day they exposed their blue-scarred bodies to the sea-air and sun, unconsciously performing the physical version of Wordsworth's mental act of storing up sublime vision for future periods of recollection:

> These beauteous forms,
> Through a long absence, have not been to me
> As is a landscape to a blind man's eye:
> But oft, in lonely rooms and 'mid the din
> Of towns and cities, I have owed to them,
> In hours of weariness, sensations sweet,
> Felt in the blood, and felt along the heart;
> And passing even into my purer mind,
> With tranquil restoration.

Then, the fortnight over, the colliers having had their annual dose of health reluctantly said farewell to the sea, sun, sand and bracing air and made their way back to the valley to carry on providing the world with coal.

CHAPTER TWELVE
Tydraw

There were three different routes to Tydraw from Trehafod. One was to take the bus to Ponty and thence up to Maesy-coed, either on the single decker or by walking up behind the County Cinema and along Sardis Road; then it was uphill on the road past the schools, the Maritime colliery (which my mother always called 'the Marentine') and Gelliwion Farm. There were two ways by which the whole distance could be walked: one over the mountain top, which was the more direct, taking about forty-five minutes and the one I preferred as it was wild, untamed and unpopulated except for sheep; and the other, which my mother preferred, probably because there were dwellings to be passed and she could have a chat on the way, and Mam loved chats.

This latter route involved going 'up the bung'lows'. It was necess-ary to walk the length of our street, often the longest part of the trip despite only having forty houses in it, because of Tump ladies' tendency to spend hours admiring the view from their doorstep. On seeing my behatted mother coming along the pavement they would smile in delight, their spirits rising as mine sank, to think she was good for at least half an hour's gossip.

"Oh, hullo, Mrs Davies. Going over the farm, are you? Shutting the shop for the day?"

"Yes, that's right, gul. Got to have a break now and then. And it's nice to go home for a change."

Tydraw was always home, a description I initially objected to and queried, as home was in Bryn Eirw shop with me and Dad, not Tydraw, but I accepted her explanation. "Well, I was brought up there, Mari fach, and as long as someone in the family lives in Tydraw, it'll be home to me. A second home, of course," she added, seeing my turned-down mouth, "but home, all the same. It'll be just the same for you when you grow up. Bryn Eirw will always be home, wherever you are."

"You don't rather Tydraw to us, do you, Mam?"

"Oh, no, my lovely. I love you best in all the world," she would say cheerily.

My possessiveness was appeased on hearing this as I required my father and me to be top of her list in everything. Although in later years regretting not having had brothers and sisters, when small I quite abhorred the idea of having any siblings and when I realised where babies came from would mentally measure my mother's stomach, surreptitiously looking at her when she was busy peeling potatoes or washing up. I wanted her all to myself and wasn't prepared to share her with anyone else other than my father.

So after several greetings of "Ow be, Mrs Davies?", enquiries about and discussions on the internal and external state of one's body, the weather past and present, popping into the odd house to see their new wallpaper or sleeping or screaming baby, we would eventually arrive at the top end of the street where there were steps up to small gardens in front of the houses. Now the road fortunately became less inhabited with only a few houses dotted around, then on either side of the cinder track a series of allotments which had reverted to nature, presenting a delightful play-wilderness of tall grasses, abandoned apple trees and rhubarb patches, brambles and a breached fence despite a gate with a rusty lock.

There was one house standing right at the top of the very steep Parish Road overlooking the river far below and if we could pass this house unseen I really felt the journey was under way. This house belonged to the Dawkins family and Mrs Felicia Dawkins, who was an insurance collector and highly entertaining, could talk the moon and stars to kingdom come. She had a quiet, introverted son, Shadwell, and a lively daughter, Cerran. There is a saying in French: "Elle ne boit pas, elle ne fume pas, elle ne drague pas — mais elle parle!" and if this applied to anyone it applied to Felicia Dawkins...

"Ooooh, 'allo, Mrs Davies. Shop shut, is it? I was just goin' to send our Cerran down for some opening medicine. Our Shadwell is constipated somethin' awful, gul, poor dab. 'E don' say much at the best of times but oh, i'ss makin' 'im awful miserable — 'e's jes' sittin' over by there, lookin' out of the window all day long, aye, an' our George do say to 'im, 'e do say, Why don' you go an' 'ave a coupla pints down the Vaughan's, Shadwell? Do you good, mun, an' cheer you up a bit it will, an' all. An' I tell you, Mrs Davies, 'e could do with a bit of cheerin' up, oh, don' talk, gul, 'e do make us all feel evil with 'im, not sayin' nothin' all the time. Jew know, 'e 'aven' spoke since yesterday. I tell you, I'm glad to get out of the 'ouse for a bit an' 'ave a change, though I got the rheumatics in my leg bad today, gul. I'ss this ol' wet weather all the time — it do get in your joints awful, don' it? An' when it do rain 'ard we 'ave a river runnin' right down the side of the 'ouse, comin' down from Woodfield, on'y 'cos the Council won' come and clear the drains, an' it makes the 'ouse damp, see? Oh, I got paper 'angin' off on the wall on that side. Oh, they make me tampin' mad, they do. I've written to them four times an' they 'aven' done nothin' about it, no. An' what do we pay our rates for, Mrs Davies? For them ol' councillors to go on trips, thass all." At this point she would gather breath and, in a sweeter tone: "Mr Davies all right is 'e? I don' s'pose 'e's keepin' the shop open for you? In work I 'spect, is he? Oh, I'll 'ave to send our Cerran down 'Afod for some Laxipurg, then."

I would wait patiently for Felicia to have her say, with my mother nodding or shaking her head furiously in agreement with her every word, as it saved time.

Then there were only the half dozen or so bungalows to negotiate, with a few greetings rather than chats, as they had big gardens in front and you had to shout. This route ran parallel to the main valley but much higher up on the side of the mountain and took us above the Tymawr colliery in Hopkinstown and towards the Western tip. We passed the shack housing Gilo and Anna Vaughan and their ten offspring, built of unrendered breeze blocks, bricks and stone with rusty corrugated sheets for a roof, along under a mound known as The Pimple with Landraw Farm off to the right, then down over the damp, reedy field of Waun y Pistyll to join the curving, tree-sheltered road to Tydraw just above Gelliwion.

I loved these walks to Tydraw with my mother who, like a true hiker, would carry my father's silver-tipped walking stick or, if she forgot that, would pick up any piece of branch to remove small stones out of her path or to lean on over a muddy patch or difficult terrain. She talked practically non-stop, only pausing in tongue and forward motion to get her breath, but these excursions were always put to good use to teach me something. On one such she decided I should learn to tell the time, so, with the aid only of a few pebbles in a circle above the Western tip and a clock face drawn with the walking stick in some grey mud a bit further on, by the time we reached Tydraw I knew it was ten to eleven and nearly time for a ginger biscuit and a cup of tea. On these walks I learned the Welsh names of the Tydraw fields, the ear-markings of the sheep owned by the neighbouring farms, the names and whereabouts of the roads and chapels in Pontypridd and some of the pubs. I had verbal tests on prices of things in the shop, the names of Mam's brothers and sisters, the types of tree we passed and some of the capitals of Europe. Mam told me about her childhood, the different clothes that were worn in the early twentieth century and when we had talked enough she would teach me songs: It's a *Long Way to Tipperary, Ar Hyd Y Nos, Charlie is My Darling, Mae Hen Wlad Fy'n Hadau, Loch Lomond* and many more, which we would sing at the top of our voices as we walked along, only moderating them when a lone hill-walker was espied, in case he thought we were drunk.

Once ensconced in Tydraw, my mother and aunt talked, in Welsh when they didn't want me to understand, and went off to the parlour to try on hats or wash the china ornaments from one or other of the dressers, went outside to feed the chickens, made cakes and tarts, gathered black and red currants, gooseberries, peas, broad and kidney beans from the garden, then would operate on them in various ways, still talking non-stop. I got bored with all this, so would go off to find one of my uncles or my cousin who would be working somewhere outside, and on finding one would plaintively ask: "What you doing? Can I come with you, Uncle Dick?"

He would look at me askance, his ever-present dog keeping close to his side, then say: "Orright, Mary. But first, go and fetch me some matches from the house, will you?"

Off I would scamper and on my return to the yard, he'd be gone. The ruse always worked and even to my plea: "You won't go then, will you, Uncle Dick? You will wait for me by there?", he would heartily answer; "Yes, yes, 'course I will". But once my anxious face looking back over my shoulder had disappeared round the corner of the house, he would too.

My cousin Gwilym was more direct with me. "What do you want to come with me for? No, I'm far too busy to have kids hanging round, getting in my way. I'm going to Pen'coedcae in any case, and it's too far for you." And off he would go, cheerily turning down my offers of assistance in his agricultural tasks.

Uncle Lewis, the oldest in the family, could usually be relied on for a bit of company. He was normally to be found in the flourishing acre garden in front of the house, doubtless aided in its fertility by the unsophisticated lavatory with its double-holed wooden seat in a little building in one corner. He tended the garden with his green fingers and a delight it was to behold, containing every salad and green vegetable, garden fruit on bushes and trees and row upon row of potatoes you could scrape with your thumb and which were as sweet and tender as the first slice of roast chicken off the breast-bone, with which they went very well. He was a calm, gentle man with a yellow moustache, a little bit of grey, wispy hair and bright blue, smiling eyes. He was unworldly wise and marvelled at the things I told him about Trehafod. He chuckled a lot and was the most interested, attentive listener ever.

It was Uncle Lewis's job to take the milk churns to the collection platform on the Castellau road the far side of the brook at the edge of Waun Cryn, and he would let me ride with him in the gambo most of the way. However, there is a hairpin bend on the Tydraw side of the steep narrow road down to the brook which is badly cambered and has a lot of loose stones on the inside bend. Just before reaching this place I had to get out and walk. Some years previously Uncle Lewis had had a nasty accident here — the pony had lost its footing, the gambo wheels had gone off the road and the whole outfit, gambo, pony, churns and uncle, had fallen fifty feet down the bank through the trees towards the stream. Lewis suffered a broken pelvis and wasn't discovered for some hours.

My mother always attended to his corns before it was time to leave and I was a curious spectator at this operation. She would get hot, soapy water for him to soak his feet in, then he would put his white, scaly, blue-veined leg, with the trousers rolled up to the knee, onto the towel on her lap. Then she would cut the nails, the hard skin and the callouses and put onto various toes corn pads, paste and plasters brought from the shop, attire the feet in clean long woollen socks and the job was done until next time.

We always left Tydraw with eggs individually and expertly wrapped in newspaper, a chunk of fat bacon, salt butter if some had been recently made, a piece of spare rib ('sperrip' my mother used to call it) if a pig had been killed, together with the liver and pig's 'apron' for Mam to transform into faggots, garden produce especially rhubarb and potatoes in season, and in my pocket I would finger a few florins from my aunt and uncles and a strip of sweet points.

The Tydraw family usually had a goose for Christmas dinner, so after one of the January visits we would return home with a jar of goose-grease with a frilly paper lid held on with string or a piece of elastic. My mother treated this with even greater reverence than she did brandy — 'the water of life' — as it was the infallible cure for a bad chest. At the first hint of a cold — a sniff, sneeze, wheeze or cough — out would come this wretched, sticky goose-grease to be spread on a strip of old flannel shirt and tied around the chest and upper back. Many nights I was put complaining to bed, smelling like a rancid chip shop as even if it were effective it did not exactly exude the sweet perfume of roses, nor was it even as pleasant as dandelions. The trouble with it was that you couldn't sleep because you had to concentrate on not breathing because of the awful pong.

There were times, such as sheep-washing, -shearing, -marking and dipping, haymaking and harvesting, when there was so much activity and excitement in Tydraw I didn't need any other diversion to fill my day. My uncles and cousin couldn't get away from me then as I knew exactly where they'd be. On such occasions they were so busy they didn't notice me around anyway and there was such a noise and bustle with dogs barking and prancing, men shouting and bustling and sheep bleating and panicking. I would try to be of some help, such as standing against a hole in a fence so the sheep wouldn't try to escape before being branded or running from the barn to the shed with a pair of shears to be sharpened. I very willingly pitched in to roll up and stack the newly washed and shorn but still greasy fleeces, until I discovered maggots in them, when my enthusiasm for that particular job died an instant death.

Endless pots of tea had to be carried out to the barn because on shearing days all the neighbouring farmers came in to help and shearing is hard, thirsty work. Huge amounts of food had to be prepared and cooked for dinnertime, and I watched in amazement as farm workers consumed their meals — plates piled with pounds of mashed potato, cabbage and meat — then mopped up the gravy with chunks of bread several inches thick, more food on one plate than I ate in a month. After a healthy helping or two of apple tart and custard and a few more gallons of tea, they'd be off unceremoniously, slapping cap on head, thumbs tucked in waistcoat pockets, to carry on with the job of pitching hay or shoving sheep.

In between these momentous events, apart from Uncle Lewis, I was left very much to my own devices in Tydraw, so after a few slides down the hay stacked in the Dutch barn, forays into lofts, stables and cowsheds, playing with the pups, kittens or pet lambs if there were any, climbing a few trees, running over the walls, chasing the angrily clucking chickens around Cae Mawr and collecting their eggs, I would explore the granary. This was a big room above the back kitchen, reached by stone steps outside the house and, untrue to its name, no grain was stored there. The floor was boarded and there was a small, low window, but with the door left open there was sufficient light to see the wonders inside: discarded crockery and small farm implements, rusty chains, broken scythe handles, hooks, ploughshares, sickle blades, sharpening stones, files. There were piles of old farming magazines, newspapers, musty, dusty books, trunks of old clothes, toys, ancient, warped, broken-stringed tennis raquets, a curved cricket bat, jam-jars containing buttons, nails and empty cotton reels, discarded feather mattresses, broken chairs, bedsteads — the list was endless.

One day, bored and idly poking around, I found under a pile of dusty, yellowed boys' comics, *Champion* or *Rover* or some such, a collection of red-bound books which all had 'William' in the title, by a man or woman with the unusual name of Richmal Crompton. After blowing and shaking off the cobwebs and specks of dirt, lime and plaster from the walls, I flicked over the thick, slightly furry pages. There were a few drawings inside of a tough, scowling boy with a turned up nose, not so much wearing a school cap as balancing it on one ear. He was dressed in a crumpled, short-trousered suit, socks corkscrewed around his ankles and with what looked like a stripey bit of bandage around his neck which no doubt originated as a tie, with above it a grimy collar, of which one wing stuck out sideways and the other had taken partial leave of the shirt. This, no doubt, was William. The particular book was entitled *William's Crowded Hours*. I pulled one of the surplus mattresses near the window and, flopping down on it, raising a cloud of dust, began to read about the wayward but ingenious William Brown and his gang of Outlaws, Ginger, Henry, and Douglas and the awful, pestering, ever-present girl, Violet Elizabeth Bott, whose pwogwession thwough life was a sewies of linked thweats to scweam until she was sick in order to get her way.

After a page I was hooked... I heard my mother calling: "Mary, Mary, where are you? Come and have some tea!" It was teatime, and I'd only just had dinner!

Before I went down to the kitchen for my banana slices suspended in red jelly with custard, gooseberry tart, home-made jam, Welsh cakes and compulsory bread and butter, I had ascertained to my delight there were a half dozen of these William books. I dusted them off, gave them a tap and promised to return.

My enthusiasm for visiting Tydraw redoubled in the following months. I didn't pester my relations any longer or aggravate the animals. No sooner arrived than I would disappear to the granary to read about William on my mattress, which was an ideal repository as there was ample room to roll around laughing on it, thus incidentally making the feathers fly out, provoking constant sneezing fits that betrayed my whereabouts.

My father visited with us when it was a weekend day. He too found the time tedious as the two sisters did jobs and chatted, often in Welsh (a language my father understood but did not speak), and he could scarcely ask the uncles if he could accompany them on their rounds, although his carpentry skills were sometimes in demand and put to good use on the farm. After dinner he and I normally went for a walk — up Gelliwion mountain, if we had come on the bus, down the brook or to Shoni's Pond, or up to the *Pen Y Frenhines* (Queen's Head) pub in Penycoedcae where he would buy me lemonade and himself beer, which we drank on a bench outside. If it was especially fine and we had a few hours to spare, we walked to Castellau and bought the drinks at the Lamb and Flag. For part of the way on this walk, over-long for little legs, he would carry me on his shoulders, an excellent habit formed on holiday one summer in the Carmarthenshire countryside around Llanstephan, where we were staying.

During the William period, I disappeared to my 'library' after dinner, and this particular day, before long, heard Dad's voice:

"Mary, Mary, come on! What about our walk?" Reluctantly leaving the warm softness of my feather bed and taking *William the Outlaw* with me, I explained I didn't want to go far that day as I was involved in William's machinations as the one and only member of the junior branch of the Society of Reformed Bolshevists to enlarge his club and find another adherent other than the next-door cat and was anxious to get back to it. Dad was as anxious to roam the country lanes. "Oh, we'll take the book and you can read it when we get to the Queen's. Or perhaps we'll have a sit down on some grassy bank on the way."

It sounded quite attractive, so along I went, but for some reason that day the road was dusty, stones kept getting in my shoes, there was nothing interesting to look at, no foxes, hedgehogs or even field voles, and my father's stories didn't hold my attention. My mind was on William's escapades and his long-suffering sister Ethel and brother Robert. A hundred yards down the road from Tydraw was a grassy bank, inviting one to rest and read, but my father was intent on exercise.

After some mumbling and grumbling on my part, we reached a compromise. He would walk along in front and I would come behind, reading the book held open in my left hand while with my right I would hang on to the tail of his jacket. This method of progression worked very well until he stopped to light a cigarette or speak to someone out for a stroll in the country, when I would carry on and flatten my nose on his tweed jacket. Walking downhill could be hazardous, too, as I tended to step on his heels and once or twice accidentally caused him to walk out of his shoe. However, apart from a few good-humoured exclamations of "Oh, Jesus. Kids!", Dad tolerated the situation and most of the William books were avidly consumed on the grassy banks and outside the local pubs as well as on the move in the lanes up and down around Tydraw. The little cortège of two and a book in single file must have presented an odd spectacle to any onlooker — like something out of *Just William*.

CHAPTER THIRTEEN
Hafod School

People born and bred in Trehafod have one thing in common — they all pass through Hafod school. My father attended at the turn of the century, forty years later I was a pupil there, and my own son, then two and a half, briefly passed through its portals thirty years later on.

Most look back with fondness on their schooldays, even if they weren't all enjoyable all of the time, and especially on those of the first ten years of life. This nostalgic affection is particularly true of Hafod school which was like a second womb — the familiar building, local teachers and of course the village children, most of whom one knew.

The school impinged on my life three times: as a pupil, then for a month as a student teacher and finally as a temporary teacher of the reception class. As far as school is concerned, distance definitely lends enchantment to the view.

Pupils I have taught, who belonged to the awkward squad for their whole school career and who were sullen, difficult, uncooperative, often aggressive and determined not to learn, greet you in later years on a chance encounter like a long lost bosom friend, pumping your arm with joyful enthusiasm, and tell you how much they had enjoyed school, although they might have been naughty now and then. They usually say they wish they had worked harder when they had the chance but are earning millions anyway.

The infants' section where children began the learning business at three years of age was in a green corrugated-iron building at right angles to the high concrete river-wall. Inside this building were four classrooms side by side and at either end was a cloakroom. Between the second and third was a glass cage for the infants' school headmistress. Her bespectacled, swivelling head on its long neck could be seen in classes two and three surveying them for any instances of miniature inattention, indiscipline or rebellion. I think the teachers of these classes were kept up to a more demanding mark than in one and four by their superior's ever vigilant eye. The first class was largely for play, with a gentle introduction to the mysteries of reading and the even greater mysteries of sums. There were assorted educational toys: lots of bricks of various kinds, deviously engineered into mind-developing games, in carts, coloured and numbered; of various shapes and sizes for fitting into boxes and for building into geometric shapes; slotted and slatted bricks, hollow bricks which fitted into other hollow bricks — the types were endless. It was not unusual for a passer-by or a neighbour living at the school end of Lewis Terrace to see one of these coloured wooden bricks come flying out through a window, hurled by a baby hand frustrated because the wretched thing refused to go into its allocated place. Whether these toys were meant to develop the children's minds numerically or to exercise them in self-control was uncertain, but they rarely appeared to give them mental fulfilment. Much howling was heard and hot, red, contorted, angry little faces witnessed. There was other apparatus for pure relaxation — slides, swings, sandpits, toy shops and Wendy houses — which the babies enjoyed but occasionally came to blows over. In the afternoons, tiny canvas folding beds were brought out of a cupboard, set up and the children put to sleep for an hour before being fetched from school by anxious mothers, daily hopeful of scholastic miracles.

"Did Davy learn his alphabet today?"

"Can Gwenllian count to twenty yet?"

The children needed this rest to get over their exertions and frustrations of the morning, and their teacher certainly needed it to prevent frayed nerves becoming permanently fringed.

Immediately out of the reception class, as it is now called, the babies' class as it then was, acquisition of knowledge began in earnest. There was no transition period, no gentle introduction to ABC and 123. Play and persuasion were over; this was the serious stuff and tantrums and tempers were no longer tolerated. If any child imagined it could pursue the prima donna act from the previous class, it was soon disillusioned with a quick smack or the cane, or, for any further disregard for authority, put outside in the cold and left to ponder the error of its outburst. And there was always the disapproving eye of the headmistress in her glass cage to contend with, and her threat to tell your mother, with further disgrace and disfavour, not to mention the horrified faces of your mates, simultaneously looking smug because it was not they being castigated. So children sat obediently in little chairs behind their own desks in orderly lines throughout the room and worked at improving their minds on the first, possibly the second, rung of the ten thousand rung educational ladder stretching before them.

During this second year was the time when children inevitably felt ill the previous night or in the morning with head-aches, tooth-aches, tummy-aches, arm-aches, leg-aches, aches anywhere, mira-culously cured once it was too late to go to school, only to return the same evening or the following morning. Mothers new to school took a few days to fathom this ruse. I got away with it once. It probably took the best part of the second year of school to get children used to what life would be like for perhaps the next sixteen years. Then the pattern was established and all was more or less plain sailing from that moment on. Words naturally got longer, numbers higher and behaviour better the further you proceeded along the corridor to the right. And there was always play-time.

No sooner had the bell rung somewhere around eleven for play-time than the building began to shake. It was a yard or so above the ground, supported on stanchions and the assembly area in front of the classrooms was boarded. Two square, similarly floor-boarded tunnels led from the assembly point down to the playground. The mini-earthquake was the result of children, most in an advanced state of eagerness for fifteen minutes' freedom, pounding over these wooden floors. Once the stampede had subsided, all was quiet once more till lunch-time as the children never stampeded back to re-start lessons. Meanwhile the teachers could enjoy a break with a biscuit and a cup of tea, apart from the poor soul on duty, who had to take her sustenance with her into the yard where she kept an eye on the mayhem and tried to dissuade youngsters from scaling the river-wall barrier and making their escape after a quick paddle across the river, shallow enough in summer.

The toilets were in separate cubicles in a row outside in the yard, about twelve for girls one side of a seven-foot stone wall, and on the boys' side a urinal open to the sky and a few lavatories. This little assemblage of buildings separated the infants' from the junior school playground. Naturally on release from class this area was the first that children with their bell-trained bladders made for, with more reluctance on winter days when flesh normally covered required exposure to the cold air. Unfortunately some builder, clearly innocent of the ways of small male children, had constructed the urinal against, not opposite, the dividing wall and squeals and shouts from little girls would be heard as they tried to dodge sporadic fountains of spray spurting from over the divide. The duty teacher, usually a woman, would sigh, stamp across to the urinal and stride in, quite unabashed, to emerge seconds later, one hand holding a cup of tea and the other frog-marching a small boy, trousers still unbuttoned and frantically trying to stow away an offending part, with the grin, as instructed, having been wiped off his face.

Being an only child of parents married in their late thirties, if not exactly spoilt, I was indulged and allowed to do more or less as I liked within reason. Doing as I liked meant being lazy and not exerting myself in school. After all, I could count up to a hundred and as it was most unlikely I'd ever have more than a hundred anything that required counting, what need had I to learn about boring concepts of HTU and LSD? My parents read to me whenever I wanted to hear stories, so why toil my brain to fathom the translation of the alphabet into words? Now and then my mother would issue a vague warning: "Little girls who don't work in school end up scrubbing the floors in the Vaughan's Arms, mind."

I didn't exactly fancy such a job for myself, but being only six or seven thought I had a year or two to make up lost time. All in all, Blanche Richards, an athletic looking lady with a firm, handsome face, the teacher of the class on the extreme right, or top infants, had a difficult time pushing back the educational barriers as far as I was stubbornly concerned. In test after test, reading and arithmetic, I came bottom or near bottom. It unjustly didn't seem to matter to her that I could race all the other kids in the class, boys included, and stay upside down longest in handstands against the river wall.

One Friday on the way home from school I had an argument with Olive Hughes, she of the overflow pipe and the early teas, as to whether London was a hundred or a thousand miles away. We saw

Mervyn the Milk in Phillips Terrace and asked his opinion. He wasn't exactly sure of the distance to the metropolis but rollicked with laughter to hear Olive thought it was a thousand miles and called her a silly billy.

"No, mun. That's China you would get to if you went that far!"

Her pride was pricked and her dignity dented, and, to spite me, on seeing my mother she said: "Mary was bottom again today, Mrs Davies, in reading and sums. She can't read, you know. I can. Miss says she's a dunce."

My mother was aghast, looking from me to Olive and back to me again, hoping for a denial which never came. Finally, in a sharp, unbelieving tone: "That's never true, Mary?"

Again, no denial, but Olive once more piped up, putting the boot in: "And Miss said, if she wasn't careful she would have to wear one of those funny dunce caps."

My mother looked dumbfounded, as though her ear-trumpet had been struck by lightning. "Did she, by Job?" was all she could manage in her shame.

This time Olive did provoke a response from me.

"Liar! Oh, you liar! She's a cleckerbox, telling lies, Mam. She didn't say that. She didn't, Mam" but by then Mam was past caring and had planned her course of action and my doomed playless weekend.

"Oh, well," she said determinedly, as my heart sank to my knees on hearing her next words, "she'll be able to read by Monday."

Dad had fish and chips from Eileen's chip shop that evening on returning from work as my mother took me through every word in every story book I owned, so that by nine o'clock I was for the first time ever desperate to retire from the fray and go to bed, never wanting to hear about Rupert Bear, Hansel and Gretel, Red Ridinghood, Christopher Robin or Jesus ever again.

Saturday and Sunday went much along similar lines between meals and I didn't even have a respite when Mam was preparing them as I had to work out what it said in the *Beano* and *Dandy* to read to her when the meal was over. School on Monday morning was a blessed release from the hardest and most prolonged few days of mental toil I'd ever known and I even thought scrubbing the floors in the Vaughan's Arms must be preferable to this torture.

However, it was with some cheer in my heart and a bouncy step I approached Miss Richards in school.

"I learned to read over the weekend, Miss. Shall I read something to you?"

It was a turning point in my life. Even sums unravelled their complications to me and when encouraged to read 'with expression' Miss said, "Well done, Mary. Your mother's done a good job, tell her." I was never bottom again, not in that class, anyway. Good old Mam.

During the early years of the war I trudged to school every day with a green square box hanging at my side, attached to a strap which went across my chest and over my shoulder. To me the box seemed large and cumbersome as the motion of walking caused it to jump and bump against my leg and when running it was even more of a nuisance as it flew round behind and bounced against my bottom. As I ran most of the time, this was a daily chastisement. The box contained nothing useful like food, fruit, toys or even books but a gas mask in case the Germans invaded Trehafod.

I hated putting the thing on my face — it had straps securing it at the back of the head and you had to go up inside it, then ease it on so that it was in the correct and secure position. It caught bits of hair and tweaked them painfully in the process and one's face was squashed in as no provision seemed to have been made for cheeks. Eyes were well accommodated as there were two enormous goggles, and as for chin, I wondered whether the makers of these contraptions hadn't sent us by mistake gas-masks for baby elephants, for hanging down in front for a good six inches was a corrugated rubbery tube similar to an elephant's trunk, ending in what appeared to me to be a jam-pot cover with small perforations in it. When the thing was in place, you looked ridiculous. Fortunately everyone was in the same boat but you couldn't laugh because, first, it was no easy matter breathing inside and the goggles got all steamed up so you couldn't see out, secondly, they were also quite useless for a game as communication was limited. Talking came out as muffled noises and the physical motion that seemed a natural accompaniment to wearing the gas-mask was a monster-type rolling one with waving arms and bandy legs. If my generation suffer from claustrophobia, then the reason is the gas-mask and having one's head incarcerated in it at daily practice.

We were puzzled at the reason for having to wear this apparatus should Trehafod be over-run with Germans, but after much discussion several explanations were put forward:

1. They made us look so ugly, the Germans would be frightened. This was the most popular theory, which I didn't subscribe to at all. I had seen pictures of these Germans in the *Western Mail* and some, called Himmler, Goebbels and Goering, not to mention Hitler with his floppy black hair and thin moustache in his screwed-up face, were uglier than the gas-masks, so how would they be scared of them?

2. The masks made us all look alike, so they wouldn't be able to tell who was who. Apparently they were going to dispose of the unhelpful and unintelligent people unless these latter made for the hills, and in the chaos of a surprise attack the anonymity of the gas-mask would confuse them as to whom to shoot.

3. They were gas-masks, weren't they? So that meant they would bring their dentists with canisters of gas and they would run around shooting gas into your face through a nozzle. This latter seemd the most likely theory to me and I trusted they wouldn't take your teeth out at the same time. That would be a bit mean. On further rumination I decided that no, teeth would be left intact, as they probably didn't have enough dentists to take out all the teeth of the Trehafod population in one day, and at night we could surely escape over the mountain. Anyway, someone would certainly bomb the train bringing them up from Ponty.

Nobody ever thought to ask the teachers what the gas-masks were for exactly, or perhaps someone did, in a complaining tone of voice, and was told not to be cheeky. Oh, I hated those Germans and the worry and trouble they caused me.

Apart from the daily practice of putting on the gas-masks, which I'm glad to say became once weekly as the war progressed and we started winning, there was also the routine of going to the air-raid shelter. This was at the top of the juniors' yard, facing the row of lavatories seventy yards away and slightly downhill, with the green corrugated shed of the infants' school twenty yards further on. The shelter was a narrow corridor incorporated in the school boundary wall, running the length of it from the pumphouse at the river end to the school's back entrance. There were three little spaced out entry porches, one at either extremity and one in the middle. Inside was damp-smelling, and as black as an unlit coal mine, with benches fixed along the walls facing each other. Children were ushered in with squeals and great reluctance, the girls hanging on to each other's cardigans and keeping close together, huddled near the open door and the light of day and as far as possible away from spiders, mice, beetles and the other horrors contained inside. Occasionally a bold boy would enter through an end door, make his way down the corridor unseen in the gloom, uttering faint ghostly noises, at which the girls would pause and listen, start to whimper and cling on even tighter to each other, before the boy, savouring the moment, would suddenly emit a loud 'Waaaah!' to send the now screaming, hopping girls scuttling back out past the startled teacher who had had so much trouble persuading them in in the first place.

It wasn't quite so bad when the lights were lit — at least you could see the spiders and mice coming at you then — but for some reason we had to practise in the dark and it was only when we were all inside and the doors shut that the lights could be put on. We tried to argue the logic of it with Miss Richards.

"But miss, you can't see the lights in the day."

"The rules say we've got to go in with the lights off, Joyce."

"Why, miss?"

"Because of the blackout, Morfydd. The Nazi planes will bomb any lights they see."

"But miss, we're not here at night. Please miss, can we have the lights on, please? 'Cos some of the boys try to frighten us in the dark."

However, no amount of protest or persuasion made the hierarchy change their minds and weekly and weakly we were despatched into the hateful place. Surely, even an invasion of German dentists with their gas-bottles would be better than this.

Each child was 'billeted' with a family in a house near to the school. When the air-raid siren, a long, wailing, snaking noise, rang out, you had to leave everything, run to the cloakroom to get the box of gas-mask, slip it around you and run as fast as you could to your billet. It sounds horribly dangerous half a century on. What about the traffic? And perverts? It was simple, as there were none. One saw the occasional van on the main road, Mr Collins's cart, the Porth-Ponty buses and now and then, to great excitement, and number-plate noting by the boys, a black car usually driven by a man in uniform. As for the other, I don't think it had been discovered then. The streets were gloriously empty, made for games: hide and seek in people's doorways and sometimes passageways, as doors were never locked and indeed normally left open; cowboys and Indians or British and Germans in the back lanes or gwlies. This latter game was very popular but very one-sided as no one would ever assume the Teutonic role. "'Ack-ack-ack! Ack-ack-ack! Ack-ack-ack! I got you! You're dead! Go on, mun, fall down. You're dead."

"No, I'm not. 'Ow can I be dead? I'm on your side, dopey."

"No, you're not. You're a Jerry. Ack-ack-ack! There you are, you're dead again now. Go on, lie down."

"I'm not, I tell you. I'm on the British side."

"No, you're not. You were picked for the Jerries."

"Snot fair! I'm not playin' then, if I got to be a Jerry."

These games usually ended in indignant argument with sometimes the keener players offering to swap sides and be the Germans themselves, but as they were the bossy and most aggressive boys, the balance was upset, the game proceeded all wrong as the Hun would win, and that was not in the plan at all.

I was billeted with the Hicks family, whose house fronted the main road next to Bethel chapel, opposite the station. It was one of the furthest billets from the infants' school apart from the houses of children who lived in the vicinity and who could run home within a certain time. I was probably allocated to this house as Mr Bert Hicks was deputy superintendent at the Sunday school and I was known to the family. The idea was to get to your billet before the siren ended because then the German bombers would come and if you weren't in the Anderson shelter by that time, you'd had your chips.

I rather liked the real air-raids as although I had to leave my coat and pixie hat behind, unless it was very wet or cold, it was a definite bonus to get out of school and set off for a little run up past Leslie James's father's shop (house-converted but not as big as ours), into the *gwli* behind the Wayne Street houses, then into the Hicks's back garden. The Anderson shelter was a semi-circular tin shack covered in clods of earth, and we, Mr Hicks if he wasn't at work, his wife,

Kitty and Anne Hicks, their daughters, the cat, Scruffy, and son, Idwal, if he too wasn't at work, huddled in this tin shed waiting for the bombs to drop. They never did, thank goodness, but we did sometimes hear the heart-stopping deeper drone of the Jerry planes, and as the noise came closer, chatting ceased and breaths were held. Actually the most frightening aspect of the whole thing was Idwal's tense face in the semi-darkness, as he had a hare-lip which distorted his mouth and nose. But he was a very amenable fellow, although I had a devil of a job understanding what he was saying, even if the family always knew. "Arw ahw ahw oy err ahw ehw." Seeing my complete bafflement, Kitty would translate: "Idwal says, Let's go and have a cup of tea and a bit of cake in the kitchen now." After a certain time the all-clear siren sounded, and you could leave the shelter and resume normal life. Sometimes for the men, who might be in pyjamas with a coat over them, this was bed, as they had worked the night shift, but all would first repair to the kitchen for the post-trauma snack. Despite repeated reminders of: "Straight back to class after the air-raid, mind!", I always stayed for a glass of Gwyn's milk and a piece of home-made fruit cake, and I was rarely last back in school.

One might wonder why the school children, who weekly rehearsed the real nightmare of the school air-raid shelter, didn't seek sanctuary there. The reason was that this was the emergency refuge, that all the children would be killed if assembled there when a bomb scored a direct hit, and then what would the teachers do?

On one occasion the whole school was enjoying play-time when a plane engine noise was heard. This was not rare, as British planes, Spitfires, Hurricanes and Wellington bombers, often passed overhead, to much cheering and waving from the schoolyard below. A few children looked up into the mottled sky, looked harder, blinked, swallowed, listened, looked again, hands shading eyes, and someone said: "There's a cross on it. Crikey! It's a Jerry!" Suddenly teachers were running, blowing whistles, shouting, frantically shepherding children to the air-raid shelter with its welcoming dark, damp safety, its harmless spiders and mice and into the comforting arms of its ghosts. There was much excitement and panic, but the solitary plane proceeded innocuously on its way, probably lost, its pilot no doubt far more terrified than we were.

145

During the final year of the Infants', the Big School, that is the Juniors', loomed larger in our imagination than it actually did in brick, a few yards across the playground, and one was constantly reminded of its imposing standards and demands in educational progress and otherwise by Miss Blanche Richards: "Selwyn, stop picking your nose. *Ach y fi*. If you do that, they won't want you in the Big School, mind."

"Get up off the floor, Raymond. Boys who like sitting on the floor won't go up to the Big School."

"And for goodness' sake do up your buttons, Albert. Do you think you can go walking around in the Big School with your trousers un-done, you naughty boy?"

"Hmm! What's this word pubbing you've got here, Marilyn? You have sponge pubbing for afters in your house, do you? I'm glad I don't have my meals there. And what's this? 'The man was found beab in deb'? You'll have to get your p's and q's sorted out before you go to the Big School, my girl!"

All these admonishments by the teacher were accompanied by covert amusement and nudges on one side, while the offender stood, moving from one leg to the other, biting then sucking his lips, screwing up his face and wringing his hands in confusion while managing to look suitably disconsolate and apologetic.

The children, and they were all of them, who managed to make it safely through to the Big School were consequently highly re-spected for the standards they had achieved, and I felt it was one more step away from scrubbing the floors in the Vaughan's Arms.

So, early one September, on the first day of the school year, a day which often to my disgruntlement fell on or near my birthday (what a birthday present!), we were marched in double file from Class Four to Standard One — up from green-painted corrugated iron to the veracious solidity of stone.

I was the first in the class to spoil my image in the Big School with the gaffe *à propos* my renomination as Mary Daffodil Davies. Our new teacher was Miss E. Roderick, a large, stately lady who often, on a fine morning, walked down to Hafod school from her house in Britannia, Porth. She was never seen walking back, probably be-cause it was uphill for part of the way, and at four o'clock, after hav-ing tried to teach us something for seven or so hours, she was no doubt far too weary. She had a full face, being able to maintain a

146

straight expression while wanting to laugh, a long nose, and black hair which formed a roll from one ear to the other going around the back of her head. She could be very fierce and frightening when someone didn't do their work well, but of all my teachers throughout my school life I became fondest of her during the ensuing four years. She had a habit of formally using your full name, thus distancing herself from the pupil and commanding the utmost respect, though there was no need for this as in those days it was truly a brave and foolhardy soul who contradicted a teacher, and there were only two identical Christian names in the class, Marilyn Williams and Marilyn Pritchard.

"Enid Morgan, haven't you forgotten something?"

"No, Miss Roderick."

"Then why are you wearing your pixie hat? We don't wear hats in class, you know, unless it's growing out of your head."

"Yes, miss. No, miss. Sorry, miss. I forgot it was on, miss."

"Take it to the cloakroom then, Enid Morgan. Quickly, please."

Or:

"Give out the poetry books, please, Sheila Payne."

Or:

"Well done, Edward Cook; ten out of ten for mental."

As the years passed, Miss Roderick, if she was extremely pleased, would call you by your first name. This was a great honour, and the majority blushed with pride. Unfortunately she never forgot my first day's inventiveness and would, much to my embarrassment, occasionally call me Daffodil. The class would erupt, then continue the joke later at play-time and during dinner-time, mimicking: "Come along, Daffodil. Drink up all your milk like a good girl"; "Well, Daffy, what a pretty yellow ribbon you're wearing today — you look just like a daffodil!" From then on my yellow ribbons were ignominiously discarded to the dolls, never to grace human hair again. One worthless boy took the joke even further: "Daffy! Huh! Dafty, more like..." which then continued to be a nickname used by the less sensitive and more unintelligent males in the class. If ever one was hoist by one's own petard!

However, classmates fortunately having the all-too-human trait of being quickly bored with a piece of imaginative ingenuity, eventually forgot the name until in Standard Four to my horror Miss Roderick announced one morning that we were going to read a famous poem, written by a man called William Wordsworth, which we would dedicate to Mary Davies, called 'The Daffodils'. Gales of merriment ensued. I swallowed and managed to force a grin, thinking 'here we go again', but despite having a daffodil-filled fortnight — drawing a picture of the scene in the poem; studying them bloom in a jug of water; reading the story of St David; studying the topography of the Lake District et al — the rest of the class had wearied of the joke, or had matured, and I wasn't over-tormented. But although later I admired Wordsworth's poetry, 'The Daffodils' was never one of my favourites. I wished I had originally had the sense to re-christen myself with some other flower, Pansy, perhaps.

Although I enjoyed school — I think most children did — it was a delightful bonus to have a day off. One naturally looked forward to the longer holidays: Christmas with all the fuss and presents; Easter and the annual new coat from Hargroves'; and the summer with its departure for some new and unexplored place by the sea. But it was those unexpected days off which gladdened the heart as does a warm February day with a cloudless sky and catkins on the trees. We were given such days off for various elections, local, county and general, as part of the school was used for voting, and wooden polling booths were installed in the building. The day before, Miss Roderick would announce: "No school tomorrow. We have a day's holiday for the local elections. Now, don't forget and come to school by mistake! Because we don't want to see you here, not even playing in the yard." This wasn't the case with the General Election, of course, as this was heralded weeks, months in advance, and despite the *Western Mail* becoming a tedious newspaper, monopolised by candidates' long, dull speeches, views and opinions, the pervading atmosphere was quite exciting. Be-bannered cars and vans with loud-speakers on their roofs and huge photographs of the particular candidate plastered over their sides, toured the streets and people ran out of their houses to watch rather than listen as it was difficult to understand the muffled speeches and exhortations to vote for that person. The candidates wore huge, coloured ribbon rosettes on their coats, red and yellow, blue and orange, which recalled the photos of my proud uncles at Tydraw with their prize cows and bulls and the various rosettes and bits of ribbon pinned up on the cowshed and stable walls.

Leaflets were continually distributed throughout the pre-election period, promising marvels for Trehafod, a new play-park for the Tump and a swimming-pool for the village, not to mention a reduction in rates, new and resurfaced roads, tip landscaping and more buses with cheaper fares. My father conscientiously read through the propaganda for the various parties, assessing their false claims and wild promises, and made a point of never entering into a political argument. In the shop he was the epitome of discretion and while not agreeing with many people's views would patiently and thoughtfully listen to them holding forth, often vociferously and excitedly, then simply say: "Mmmm" or "Aah, so that's what you think, is it?" or simply nod, not so much in agreement as to show he was considering the political point. His dictum was that the customer was always right and he certainly didn't want to lose any by opposing, exposing or even criticising their views. I believe he was truly a floating voter who never imposed his political ideas on anyone, ideas which were intelligently and unbiasedly arrived at, if perhaps sometimes a little cynically.

My mother was altogether a different basket of bees. She became very impassioned at the General Election and as far as possible father used to try to keep her out of the shop. If she became involved in a political argument, not only would she not be seen for several hours, but also the customer might well not be seen in the shop again for several months, perhaps years, perhaps never. Politically my mother was a mess as her heart had several affiliations. Basically she was a Liberal. "I was brought up in the country and all farmers are Liberals. And so am I," she would say. But then she also spoke Welsh, rarely if she could help it went out of Wales, and the rise of nationalism in the 'fifties imbued and enthused her with its spirit. On the other hand, she had lived through the war and Winston Churchill had been appointed leader of the nation on her forty-fourth birthday, 10 May 1940. She listened enthralled to his war oratory, often weeping tears of pride to be British. Indeed, he so inspired patriotism in her, she invested five hundred pounds in War Bonds to help the war effort, bonds practically worthless today. If only she had bought property...

What she was not, was Labour. And as ninety-nine per cent of Rhondda people are, father's desire to keep his politically naive but passionate and straight-speaking wife out of the shop at election time was a sensible one.

When voting day arrived, my mother could well have given her X to several candidates, as in local elections she also supported the Independent or Ratepayer. Her choice was happily made less difficult by there normally being no Liberal candidate, so the decision was usually a straight one between two, the Nationalist and the Conservative. I think it depended on their looks. One year the Nationalist candidate was the licensee of the Britannia Arms, near Porth, a pub my father frequented every year on Christmas night, and to my mother's amazement he announced he was going to put up a poster in the shop window supporting this very agreeable fellow. This had never happened before as he had always told my mother: "We are not having a Conservative poster in the window, Sal. It'd be madness. You put a Tory poster up, and the next thing would be a brick through the glass." Presumably patriotism prevented the populace from pitching a brick at the Nationalist. Anyway, Mam was quite happy to have the licensee's pleasant face smiling in front of the raspberry ruffles and Merrymaid toffees and would plunge into the fray of shop political discussion extolling his superiority and worthiness. However, he was not as handsome or boyish as the Tory candidate.

The great day arrived. Father voted Welsh Nationalist. Mam set off for the polling booth in the church vestry opposite, full fuss, juggling names in her head, ostensibly to vote Welsh Nationalist, privately intending to vote Conservative, but in the excitement and confusion getting the names muddled and ending up voting Labour because she couldn't remember which was which. Perhaps what an old fellow said to Meic Stephens, one-time Nationalist candidate in Merthyr, when canvassing: "To your face, they're all behind you; but behind your back they're at your throat" partially sums up my mother's dilemma as far as politics was concerned. She would have approved of proportional representation; then she could have voted for everybody. Well, most, anyway.

Going to school was a fairly straightforward process as I rarely left the house until the last minute and discovered at an early age the mathematical principle that the shortest distance between A and B is a straight line. In fact the river got in the way of the straight line,

150

so of necessity a few bends were added as well. I ran down the steep, rough Church Hill, developing nimbleness with familiarity so I reached the main road in seconds and could have drawn a map of the hill showing the position of the loose pebbles, grass patches, big boulders, impacted earth, the areas holding water after rain and, half way up, the path across to the colliery under-manager's house in Pleasant View.

Once in Phillips Terrace I hurdled the ash-buckets placed outside the houses a suitable distance apart and conveniently lined up in a row at the edge of the pavement. Then over the bridge past a few shops and houses where the main road curved, then sharp right opposite the station and so into school.

Scarcely was there time to play hopscotch or touch when a hand-bell was rung by one of the lady teachers wearing a flowery overall. There were no men on the staff then. They were probably all away at war. The pupils lined up in a lower area from the main yard, then filed in to their classrooms. The day began with prayers: 'Hands together, eyes closed' was the first command of the day, so ritual it was always mechanically intoned in a level, unvaried voice. Sometimes during the Lord's Prayer Miss Roderick's voice would ring out: "Stop! Stand up straight and don't shuffle about, Royston Hamer. David Albert Davies, stop peeping through your fingers. Right, carry on! Thy will be done on earth as it is in heaven..."

From after prayers, which also included a Jesus story, until five minutes to playtime, we did sums: HTU, LSD, YFI (yards, feet and inches), GQP (gallons, quarts and pints), HMS (hours, minutes and seconds), addition, subtraction, division, multiplication, ratios, squares, cubes, percentages, fractions, decimals and the ever-present tables. We started with the latter and every day chanted through from Two Times to Twelve Times. Then it was on to the problems: trains approaching each other at different speeds, which like the incline trams never crashed, or the men building walls, later to be joined by more men to speed up the operation, sometimes with different sized bricks. I often wondered what the final building was like — probably leaning over, like the Tump houses, with all this varying brickery and men coming and going when and as they wished — if indeed the construction was ever finished. I had the strange feeling these people were doing their bit of masonry simply to tease innocent, childish minds. Some days we would be off shopping: for forty-eight eggs at 6d a dozen; 50 bottles of sauce at 1/- each; and other enormous amounts of lard, cabbage, matches and jam. No one ever explained how we would struggle home with such massive purchases, and the number of bus trips necessary to transport these acquisitions would far outweigh their cost in bus fares. Still all this was useful for potential hotel-keepers and caterers, I supposed.

Then there was the water, clearly the main obsession of mathematicians. We were always having to fill baths with water and find out how long it would take to drain out or go cold. As if it mattered! You just had to pull the plug and it gurgled out, or if you had a tin bath, like us, you simply threw out the water in one fell gush. You didn't have to time it. If for example you had a bus to catch, it was more important to know how long your hair took to dry after the bath so you wouldn't catch cold going out with damp hair. The dirty water could look after itself — unless of course it was some devious way of detaining you to clean out the bath afterwards, a job usually done by mothers. I was amazed at how many taps dripped and cisterns leaked in these sums to further obfuscate the situation. And if sums reflected life, it was surprising that all plumbers weren't millionaires.

I didn't mind fitting carpets, as I could imagine this being a useful piece of knowledge one day, once the war was over, when carpets were being made again and were available for purchase.

Some time during the morning, a crate of small bottles of milk would be lugged into the classroom, heads counted and some bottles added or removed. This was never my favourite tipple but was decidedly more delectable in summer despite the fact that the milk was lukewarm. In one corner of the classroom under the window-wall was a large black stove with a door which devoured buckets of coal to heat the room in winter. At the top of the stove a large pipe took the smoke and noxious fumes and gases out through the wall near the ceiling. At the front of the monster heater a metal guard prevented pupil access and possible mischief. In winter, daily, to everyone's dismay, the crate was relieved of its bottles which were then placed round the guard to warm the milk. Hot milk was all right; mixed with chocolate powder it was decidedly good; lukewarm it was just tolerable; but warm, with uninviting yellow globules of fat floating around in it looking like jaundiced eyes, it was horrible. However, it had to be drunk, as you weren't allowed out to play until your third of a pint had been disposed of. So children swallowed a few times to get their throat muscles practised and supple, depressed the hole in the cardboard top, which was pulled out, and, taking a deep breath, drank the lot in one go, some usually finding its way down outside one's neck.

The class returned from play to an hour's session of mental arithmetic or poetry, or once in an aeon it seemed, when the weather was right, not too hot or cold, and Miss Roderick was feeling physically energetic, drill. This was a great treat and seemed an extended but organised playtime. We stood in rows and did exercises, together but never in unison, jumping feet apart and extending arms level with shoulders, often hitting the next person in the eye. Then we had to lean forward and touch our toes a few times. Miss Roderick always voiced, never demonstrated her instructions. If we were well behaved and uncomplaining we were allowed competitive team-games, throwing bean-bags over our heads, the last one running to the front and the rest shuffling backwards until the original leader was back in his place. Pile-ups always occurred as some dozy children would be watching the other teams or waving to a friend peeping out of a classroom window and of course the bean-bag was rarely caught.

"Aw, miss, tell Valmai! She's not playing properly. She's looking over there and making us lose."

Valmai would swipe the complainant over the head and retaliate: "How can I go backwards, *twp*, when you're standing on my feet? Gerroff, you great elephant."

Sometimes we jumped through hoops held by one of the team, normally resulting in more argument and grazed knees, and we always ended by running from the middle of the yard to touch the air-raid shelter, river and toilet walls, then back to the middle. By this time Miss Roderick had had enough fresh air, exercise and moans and it was back to class to sing a few songs such as *John Peel* and *Clementine* until the bell for dinner.

Usually after play we did mental, which few pupils liked. Miss Roderick called out various combinations of figures to be manipulated according to different mathematical principles and we had to write down the answers. It was so easy to get left behind and you daren't relax your concentration for a second or you'd get 0 out of 10, 20 or 30 and your knuckles rapped with a ruler for your pains

— and that particular castigation was painful. My father however assured me it was vital practice for serving in the shop — the mental, that is, not the knuckle-rapping, although the latter must have been useful to develop tough hands for the customers who knuckle-knocked on the counter, shouting: "Shop!"

Once a week we read poetry, a great relief from mental although most of the boys said it was cissy and I must confess to finding some parts — such as "Then hey nonny-nonny" (repeated) — silly myself, if not cissy, because it didn't appear to me to mean anything. I also didn't like expressions such as "oh sweet contentment, oh punishment, oh sweet". If you went around saying that "oh" business to anybody, they would think you were mental. Apart from these trite phrases though, poetry came a close second to drill in my estimation. If you had a good poem like 'The Highwayman' by Alfred Noyes (any relation to the fruiterer's shop outside Ponty market, Town Hall entrance, I wondered?) which was my favourite, you had a good story which formed pictures in your mind's eye, and which didn't take long to read. Also it was rather clever the way the writer not only made it sound so nice with rhymes and things, but also you could actually hear the horse clip-clopping up to the old inn-door in the moonlight. It was only a pity it was so tragic at the end, with Bess having to pull the trigger on herself. My sympathies were definitely not with the law on that occasion. The shorter poems all seemed to be about the sea. There was 'Sea Fever', a very romantic poem, deemed cissy by the boys, and another called 'Cargoes' with marvellous sounding words such as "quinquireme of Nineveh from distant Ophir", "cinnamon" and "gold moidores". Miss Roderick in a melancholy voice read to us the poem 'Annabel Lee', who was killed by a chill wind over the sea and 'The Three Fishers' by Charles Kingsley with the lines: "For men must work and women must weep/And there's little to earn and many to keep", and their reward is death, too. A certain Mr Cunningham wrote 'Song of the Sea', certainly reminiscent of 'Sea Fever' but redeemed from soppiness (one line I'm afraid was "Oh for a soft and gentle wind") by a memorable line in each of the three verses which the whole class joined in to read: "And bends the gallant mast, my boys" (verse 1); "And white waves heaving high, my lads" (verse 2); and finally in verse 3: "The wind is piping loud, my boys". There were more sea poems: 'The Moon is Up' (Noyes the Fruiterer again), every verse

154

ending with "Beyond the Spanish Main"; and the really sad poem which affected me acutely, about Mary going to call the cattle home across the sands of Dee, and true to Mr Kingsley's form, he had her trapped and drowned by the tide. I was glad there was only the brook over Tydraw.

The children often wondered why Miss Roderick read so many sea poems, and the mystery was solved when someone's mother said her boy-friend was in the Navy, on one of the battleships in the Atlantic Ocean. Afterwards on poetry days and sea poems there was much nudging and giggling, to Miss Roderick's puzzlement, I'm sure. Whatever the facts, she never married her sailor-boy, or anyone else, for that matter.

Other class favourites, at least as far as the girls were concerned, were 'The Owl and the Pussycat', 'John Gilpin's Ride' and 'Matilda' (Who Told Lies and was Burnt to Ashes) while the boys typically deigned to laugh at 'Sir Smasham Uppe' and 'Albert and the Lion' — anything that was violent or cruel. I was touched by Leigh Hunt's poem called 'Abou Ben Adhem' (May His Tribe Increase) which we first came upon after prayers as a replacement for the Jesus story. It bewitched me with all the conversation in it, making talking sound poetic:

> "What writest thou?"—
> The vision raised its head
> And with a look made of all sweet accord
> Answered, "The names of those who love the Lord."
> "And is mine one?" said Abou."Nay, not so,"
> Replied the angel. Abou spoke more low
> But cheerly still; and said: "I pray thee then
> Write me as one who loves his fellow men."

He was justly rewarded in the end by coming top of God's list, and all was well with the world.

On poetry days the mid-day bell was sadly rung all too soon, and it was time to go home for dinner and quickly adjust to the banalities of life again after tasting the realms of fantasy.

I tried school dinners (a shilling per week) in Standard One but didn't get on with them at all. Anyway, I preferred going home to see my mother at mid-day, who would often make chips for me to eat or a dried egg omelette and I didn't like missing any activities in the shop or travellers visiting the house. Besides, on Tuesdays the *Beano* or the *Dandy* was delivered with the morning paper, and I pored eagerly over the adventures of Desperate Dan, Marmaduke, Lord Snooty, and his gang, Pansy Potter, the Strong Man's daughter, Korky the Cat and Keyhole Kate before returning to school.

On Thursdays the *Girls' Crystal* magazine arrived with the *Western Mail* and more poring was done over egg and chips as I read about girls with names like Fiona, Fenella, Georgina, Drucilla and Antonia, who had adventures in schools with names like Abbeyfield, The Towers, Tall Chimneys or Marston House, and whose world was so unlike mine they could have been on Saturn. Swimming and diving teams figured prominently in these stories and the best girl was always kidnapped, put into detention or crocked an ankle prior to an important competition. There were two outcomes: either the star appeared at the last moment to win the match for the house or school despite her handicap; or a hitherto rejected girl would turn up trumps and totally unexpectedly carry off the cup, ensuring future enduring popularity and candidacy for Head Prefect. Sometimes there were ghosts and Camilla or Monica would ingeniously solve the mystery, sometimes fires in the school, and Dorothea would risk her life for the sake of her fellow pupils and Miss Fanshawe, and sometimes the beautiful though young Arabella, haughty but misunderstood, would be a top class mannequin, famous in the fashion world. Any boys that existed in the pages of the *Girls' Crystal* were elder brothers called Henry, Charles (or Chas), Theo, Lionel, Rupert and Giles, and, if they had left Daneborough, Rustington College or Elm Court, were at Cambridge, don't y'know.

At ten past one my mother would send me back to school, where the afternoon syllabus was invariably English. A few times in the year we might have instruction in something approaching history or geography but this was usually a spin-off from some other piece of instruction or knowledge. Guy Fawkes and his story always appeared at the beginning of November, as did Dewi Sant at the end of February. From a poem with the repeated line: "The Pinta, the Nina and the Santa Maria" we learned of the exploits of the discoverer of the Americas and were urged to remember for future use:

> In fourteen ninety two
> Columbus sailed the blue

One day the class trooped out into the hall to look at a picture of two small boys listening to a man in strange dress, with a ruff collar around his neck like a circus dog, who was sitting on a low sea wall, pointing into the distance. This was Sir Walter Raleigh, the story of whose cloak held the girls rapt while the boys were more interested in his potatoes and tobacco. On the opposite wall a reproduced painting depicted a bearded man in equally odd dress leaning forward with a ball in his hand, playing bowls on a cliff top while in the distance ships were approaching. Miss Roderick's answer on being questioned about this was: "Oh, that's Sir Francis Drake and the Spanish Armada. They're for next month."

Geographical instruction was imparted in much the same way, perhaps even more haphazardly.

"Fair stood the wind for France," someone might read from a poem.

"Where's France?" Miss Roderick would say.

"Across the sea, miss, next to Germany."

"Not sea. English Channel. And what language do they speak there?'

"French, miss," we chorused. And that was Europe dealt with.

We did once attempt a tracing of Australia, which turned out upside down and back to front or totally unrecognisable, so we sang 'Waltzing Matilda' instead and learned more from the song than the map.

Someone brought a foreign stamp to school with strange writing on it, and on further examination Miss Roderick declared it to be from China or Japan, where the people have slanty eyes. However, its owner declared that Miss was looking at it the wrong way up and his uncle said it was from Turkey. I didn't think Miss Roderick could have been highly qualified in geography, but you couldn't be good at everything.

Any science we did — observing tadpoles grow and drawing them in the early stages (they mysteriously disappeared when they began to assume a froglike appearance) — was done in the morning. We also drew buds but they invariably wilted before they flowered, despite constant attention, watering, wiping, bandaging when the stalk broke and warming by the fire when it was cold. Catkins or pussy-willow were popular, being reliable plants which lasted a long time, so we were expert artists at portraying catkins.

Languages, in our case Welsh, were also designated morning subjects. There was a flurry of activity in Welsh once a year for our St David's Day concert, when not only *Mae Hen Wlad Fy'n Hadau* was sung but also *Calon Lân* and *Sospan Fach* and once a small group shyly, hesitatingly, stumblingly and with much twisting of hands behind backs, sang:

> Pwsi meri Mew
> Ble collaist ty dy flew
> Wrth fynd ir rhwyn tew
> Yn yr eira mawr a'r rhew

On March 1st the girls wore daffodils and the boys leeks, which diminished in size during the morning as their wearers felt pangs of hunger. Where possible the children wore something approaching a Welsh costume, but as clothes were rationed and unnecessary garments such as tall Welsh hats not readily available in wartime, the costumes were itemised — one girl might have a red skirt, another a white, frilly blouse or a black and white checked apron. Mothers attempted to glue together pieces of blackened cardboard for the hat, but these were often lopsided, unbalanced creations that fell or sometimes sprang apart at the seam, flying up in the air or across the room, causing amusement to onlookers but distress, discomfort and ridicule to the wearer.

Because I had broken my left arm when trying to fly at three, my mother thought any pursuit that exercised the thin, bent, pathetic limb was good and would strengthen it, so I had piano accordion (as well as piano, swimming, tap-dancing and ballet) lessons. On St David's Day the Hohner Verdi III 120-bass accordion in its big, black case with the bulge on one side was hauled down to Hafod school (on the bus for two stops, if it was raining) for my recital. I didn't look forward to these occasions as I had to practise the songs so as not to look a fool in front of my class-mates by playing the wrong notes. Being the centre of attention, or at least my accordion, wasn't a role I cherished either, and children would poke at the keys and buttons and wonder that no sound issued forth. After my explanation they would plead with me to operate the bellows while they depressed the keys and sudden belching or hooting noises would erupt, making them recoil in alarm. Then when the music stand was erected at a certain moment and a chair placed in position, I would put the accordion on, my arms going through long leather straps which needed tying together with ribbon behind my back, and get on with my performance. I only knew one Welsh song, *Men of Harlech,* so played that every year, and the other tunes had to be the ones I was learning at the time: *Drink to Me Only With Thine Eyes, The Rose of Tralee, Daisy, Daisy, Give Me Your Answer, Do* — nothing to do with Wales or Welsh, but nobody seemed to mind. The assembled classes applauded me generously, mistakes or not, and I was always relieved when it was over for another year.

I must have been a sight to behold behind this huge instrument, a thin, stick-like girl with a puny left arm, my head only visible from the eyes up as I peeped over the top of the accordion at the music, with my hair, to my annoyance, and at my mother's insistence, having been specially curled in rags for the occasion. Once one of the boys ungallantly proclaimed, "Aargh! She don't know 'ow to play it proper! You're supposed to stand up to play one of them things, not sit down." However, I had tried, but the accordion being too heavy, my knees buckled, I fell over, was pinned down and had to be helped up onto a seat and rescued from the clutches of the thing. After the celebrations, though, we did have the afternoon off, and the headmistress, Miss Lally Davies, gave me and the accordion a lift back home in her car.

Ninety-nine per cent of our afternoons were dedicated to English. We learned endless proverbs and their meanings, which sometimes became confused in young minds especially when the metaphors were similar. One emerged as: 'An egg in the hand is worth two in the basket', which sounded more like an encouragement to kleptomaniacs than the moral axiom it was intended to be. Similarly, its other half was remembered by one pupil in a test as: 'Don't put all your birds in the same bush', which though not quite what Miss Roderick wanted might conceivably be good advice to the aviary department in a zoo.

It was vitally necessary to learn collective nouns as you never knew when a coven of witches, a pride of lions or a bevy of beauties might

159

come in handy. Likewise, opposites and masculine and feminine versions figured highly on the English syllabus, and we ploughed through endless nobles and their titles from King and Queen and down through the hierarchy of their unsmiling families to the lowerarchy of the Baronet and his Lady. Though titled people were not exactly commonplace in Trehafod, we were prepared for all emergencies and no animal and his mate or young escaped our exercise books, despite our never even having seen the majority of them. But how, I wondered, could you tell the difference between a cob and a swan or a hare and a leveret, and more importantly, why would you need to? We learned that black was likened to night, coal, pitch or a raven, thinness to a rake and dullness to ditchwater. I disagreed with the last, as you never knew what delights, living or otherwise, you might find in an old ditch filled with water. That portion of the environment could be most interesting. I assumed the authors had made a mistake and it was meant to be dish-water. Anything remotely connected with any form of housework was infinitely dull. Words with identical sounds but dissimilar spellings and differing meanings were explored, as were different words with the same meanings — synonyms.

Some afternoons we wrote compositions, descriptive pieces about 'My Favourite Room', 'The Market' or pages of imaginative writing on 'A Day in the Life of a Penny' or 'Myself as a Cat'. What with learning when and how to use its and it's, their and there, who and whom, and how to distinguish a verb from a noun, from an adjective, from an adverb, our skills in English were honed, preparing us for the target of the Scholarship Exam and the herculean goal of obtaining a place at the revered County School.

"Alfie Passey, what is the noun from soft?"

"Softness, miss."

"Good. Rita Robbins, what is the verb? To..."

"To — to soften, miss."

"Right. Good girl. Ben Button, the adverb is...?"

"Ummm."

"Come on, Ben Button. I went down the corridor on tiptoe..."

"...and out through the door?"

"No, no, you silly boy. Oh, that's just your wishful thinking, that is. It's not home-time yet. Softly. Softly is the adverb. It tells you how you do things. The adjective is a good description of you, isn't it, Ben Button?"

"Yes, miss."

"What is it, then?"

"Ummm. Ummm."

"You don't know, do you, Ben Button?"

"Yes miss: *naughty*, miss."

"Yes, Ben Button, naughty as well. You're soft, boy, soft."

And so it went on, education with some mock horror, humour and irony on the part of the teacher, providing the class with a bit of amusement at the expense of most of the children in turn, building character and personality in the give and take of the school situation, providing us with an insight into the ways of the adult world.

We naturally had story-books and read, or were encouraged to read round the class 'with expression', but preferred Miss Roderick to read aloud when we could all relax and enjoy the tale. The trouble with reading with expression was that you had to concentrate so hard on the words and the commas and question marks, you had no idea what the story was about.

Every evening for the final two junior school years the scholarship class had ten sums for homework and I offered up prayers of thanks in St Barnabas that the International Correspondence Schools had prepared my father so well in the various forms of arithmetic as it gave him a solid background to help me with my homework. Some evenings, when the gallons of water in the hypothetical bath were obstinate and wouldn't work out into neat cubic feet, or the trains going in opposite directions ran out of steam and were ridiculously slow, giving unacceptable answers, I would go to bed, leaving him to finish my homework, which I would hastily write up the following morning before school. Poor Dad. After a day's labours at the test beds, a few hours' shop-keeping, and all the little household tasks of putting out the ashes, fetching the coal for the fire and chopping sticks, he had the scholarship exam to prepare for. He really did deserve me to pass!

English homework was hardly ever given, as sums made up the higher percentage of exam marks, but when it was set it was almost a bonus, not an onerous task at all, as it could be quickly dispatched, unlike sums, which took all evening, so there was little chance of going out to play. As well as homework, there was piano or piano accordion practice (the instruments fortunately not learned simultaneously), longer and more desperate the day before the lesson.

One summer I also had swimming lessons after school, basically to strengthen my puny left arm rather than to prevent my drowning, but this weekly excursion to Ponty baths was a treat, I always having been of a sporty bent. The lesson always took place whatever the weather, and as it was on an evening when the pool was used only for teaching, I was the sole (non-)swimmer in the water. First, after I had changed into my bathers, Mr Thomas, the handsome, bespectacled instructor with black, wavy hair, always dressed in slacks and a stripey vest, would tutor me in the breast stroke movements. This I did, lying on my stomach on a wicker stool which prickled my tummy through my costume, and Mr Thomas held my ankles and energetically made me perform breast stroke kicks while my arms flailed wildly in front, trying to keep up with the legs. Then, after putting around my waist a rope on the end of a pole, with a flat rubber section for the stomach, I had to jump into the three-foot section — no going gingerly down the steps — and execute the strokes in the water. Meanwhile, Mr Thomas walked around the edge of the pool, holding the pole over the water with me on the end of the rope like a fish dangled on the end of a line. Eventually the frantic flapping of the water and the swallowing of gallons of chlorinated pool worked — no doubt the density of water inside was the same as that outside — and I was afloat. At such times Mr Thomas surreptitiously removed the rope, although he continued to hover above, so I would swim unaided for a few feet until I realised the rope had gone and promptly sank to the bottom, struggling up with much spluttering and coughing. After a few weeks I could swim, after a splashy fashion, but sometimes pretended I had forgotten in case the classes should be discontinued.

Another arm strengthener was considered to be playing the piano, and after making some enquiries my mother found a peripatetic teacher, Miss Joy Clarke from Pontypridd, who would come to the house to teach me for an hour after school each Tuesday. I fully expected to be playing and transposing the little tadpoles on the sheet music and manuscripts into beautiful sounds in a matter of weeks. My disappointment was great and my enthusiasm for music plummeted when after months the Kaps appeared to wince, still being subjected to the most awful, humiliating cacophony of wrong notes and chords struck in error with over-long hesitancies and pauses in between, as my stiff, short fingers jumped around the keyboard and my overtaxed brain struggled with minims, crotchets, quavers and semi-tones. Where was the flowing music my father played? His explanation: "It takes years of learning and practice, love, especially scales. Practising scales makes your wrists supple and your fingers nimble, you see" did no more than put gloom into my heart, but my mother, who could be an unflinching martinet at times, wouldn't hear of my giving up.

I was quite pleased, therefore, to hear of Miss Joy Clarke's impending marriage and her matrimonial duties' precluding any further peripatetic activity on her part. She was a piano-accordionist by profession, a champion soloist to boot, and henceforward she and her husband, Stuart Butler, a saxophonist, would only teach those instruments from their music shop in the Arcade as they had no piano on the premises. My glee was short-lived however as I watched Mam's face and read her train of thoughts: "Mmm. A piano-accordion. That's quite a bulky instrument, good for puny arms. Yes, Mary shall learn the piano-accordion, despite the inconvenience of having to take her and the instrument to Ponty on the bus each week..."

"Oh, no need to lug the accordion down each week, Mrs Davies. We'll have spare ones in the shop. And Mary can come down on her own then."

My pleading gaze had no effect on my mother as my future was decided in a few sentences and playless evenings loomed ahead. One proverb I had learned: 'All work and no play makes Jack a dull boy", nobody seemed interested in. So piano-accordion lessons were pursued for some years and became reasonably enjoyable, the initial difficulty in learning music having been dealt with on the piano. I even passed the first four examinations of the Royal College of Accordionists. All went fairly well until Joy Clarke (she kept her maiden, professional name) decided it was time for me to join the junior accordion band which practised, horror of horrors, on a Saturday afternoon. This was a sacrosanct time when my father went to watch Pontypridd RFC play their home matches in Ynys-angharad Park. He took me with him, and had done since I was three years old. Despite tearful protestations, band practice became a Saturday afternoon ritual for the summer months and I acquiesced in a docile manner while working out my plan of action for the winter. I had been making enquiries among my friends and got them to ask their parents if there was a piano teacher in Trehafod or nearby and to my great joy I discovered in Bethesda Street a Mrs Thomas, a former chapel organist, who took a few pupils. As the rugby season approached I began to sit wistfully at the piano and play a few chords. I would say to my father, making sure my mother was in earshot: "I wish I could play the piano like you, Dad. Will you play something for me, please?" He rarely had time, so I would mope around the kitchen, staring, I hoped, with pianoforte nostalgia up at the mountain, and sadly hum my old piano tunes. Eventually I broached the subject of Mrs Thomas: "There's a piano teacher down Bethesda Street, Mam."

"You don't want piano lessons as well as accordion, do you?"

"No, no. I thought I could go back to the piano, 'cos it's not getting played and it's going out of tune."

"You mean, you want to drop the accordion because you have to go twice a week and piano would be only once a week."

"Well, I was jes' thinking it would be cheaper for you, paying twice a week, and all that bus fare... Come on, Mam."

"Well, we'll see."

True to her word, Mam did see. I gave up accordion lessons and joyfully trotted down to Mrs Thomas in Bethesda Street to restart piano lessons. The only trouble with her was that she wanted to give value for money and the hour would go on for an extra thirty minutes, but I didn't mind as it was far preferable to Saturday afternoon. We had a break for a snack and a chat at half time and she was never cross with me for not practising.

After my abortive attempt at flying at three years of age left me with a greenstick fracture of the left elbow, I was packed off to the Prince of Wales Hospital in the Parade in Cardiff, because Matron Miles, who originated from Penbwch Farm near Penycoedcae, had been a friend of my mother's since childhood. The arm was repaired but permanently curved. I didn't mind overmuch because as a result of this I could put my left elbow around my head behind my right ear and for several years this was my only claim to fame. My mother was obsessed with building up the offending limb, though, via extracurricular lessons and the first of these when I was four were tap-dancing and ballet with a middle-aged, nimble lady from Penarth with hair so black it had a purple glow, who went by the name of Madame Beaton. Unfortunately, during my six weeks in hospital I had been completely isolated from my parents. They were allowed to see me — peeping through the ward windows and visting when I was asleep — but not I them. Medical thinking in the late 'thirties asseverated that youngsters would only pine and yearn for home if reminded of it, thus hampering a cure, so relatives were *personae non grata*.

This prolonged separation clearly had a profound effect on me. I was bewildered and miserable and told them in the Prince of Wales my name was Shirley as if all this was not happening to Mary Davies but to some other little girl. I developed a stammer in my speech which remained with me to a certain degree right through adolescence and even now temporarily reminds me of its former hold if I am depressed, lacking in confidence or excited.

My apparent abandonment by my parents while I was in hospital had the effect of completely spoiling my dancing lessons a year or so later. The teacher was sympathetic, despite her awesome name; the other little girls were friendly; I was a loose-limbed child; I had a pretty purple dancing dress like all the others and silver tap-shoes with a metal half-sole which tinkled on the floor as well as a tutu with a satin bodice and pink ballet shoes; but I was desperately unhappy. The lessons were held in a large room upstairs in Market Chambers in Pontypridd, where my mother would deposit me while she went off to do some shopping and other business, and I was terrified she would forget all about me and not come back. After the first fifteen minutes my eyes were constantly on the door and if she were not the first mother to came to collect her offspring I would dissolve into tears and weep inconsolably until she arrived. I must have been a dreadful nuisance to Madame Beaton, unsettling the class and needing almost constant attention. The assistant dance mistress would hold my hand but to no avail: the tears flowed. Nobody could understand what on earth was the matter with me, and I couldn't explain as I didn't know myself. Before each lesson I felt sick and developed stomach aches and pleaded to be allowed to stay home.

After a year or so, but not before my appearing in the pantomime, *Dick Whittington*, in the Town Hall as one of Madame Beaton's Troupe of Tap-Dancers, my mother realised the lessons were serving little purpose. They were discontinued and my psychological traumas, only understood years later, were over.

I had my first brush with romance in Standard One at Hafod school and initially wasn't impressed with the experience. A skinny, gangly lad called John Owen, with mousy, floppy hair, always dressed in grey — grey short trousers, grey shirt, grey pullover, grey jacket and grey socks — seemed continuously to be on the fringes of our little group of girls as we played, ran or chatted, and, in chasing games involving a larger crowd, he always ran after me. One day I let him catch me and as he held on to my arm he said: "Mary, will you go with me?"

This was an expression whose meaning was unknown to me, so I blinked and answered: "Go where?"

"Oh, you know: go with me. Jes' go with me."

"Don't be so daft. I'm not going with you if I don' know where you're goin'."

"Well, come with me down the side of the Infants' school" (there was a narrow gap between the Infants' school and the river wall) "and I'll give you a sweet."

So I followed John unsuspectingly along the gap, thinking we had to be isolated because he didn't want to be pestered by the others for his sweets, and probably feeling a sense of pleasure being the chosen one.

"If I give you a sweet, will you give me a kiss?"

This request was totally unexpected, as my experience of boys hitherto was one of loud noise, coarseness, roughness and a desire to wrestle and fight, certainly not cuddling and kissing.

"A kiss? What for?"

"Well, I like you. You're a good runner."

"What sort of sweets?"

"Jellies."

Then, after some consideration: "Mmm. Orright then."

One might think that a small girl living in a shop selling confectionery didn't need to kiss boys for sweets but it was still war-time, when such delicacies were on ration, and I was never allowed to

166

take sweets to school. If I ever had sweets in school it was because I had smuggled some money and sweet points out of the house and bought some in Greasy Mary's shop by the bridge, and it was such a palaver it wasn't worth the effort.

So I stood with my lips pursed and eyes shut, screwed up in distaste, as John planted cold, rough lips on mine for what seemed an unnecessarily long time. "Come on, that's enough," I said, backing off.

"Oh, come on, gi'ss another one."

"No, I'm not. One sweet, one kiss."

"Will you give me another one tomorrow?"

"I dunno. Depends."

"What sweets do you like best?"

"Turkish Delight chocolates."

"Oh" (in a somewhat discouraged tone). "I'll see if I can get some of them, then."

I don't think he did and I certainly wasn't sorry, as though I liked him — he was funny, nice to girls and made you laugh, unlike the majority of boys, and didn't have a green-runny nose — I didn't enjoy getting too close to the opposite sex, who had rough-textured clothes, didn't smell as nice as girls, scratched, and certainly weren't cuddly, soft and warm to kiss like Mam.

Once a term the school was visited by the nit-nurse and the order: "Heads on desks! Don't look up until told" was given. Presumably the latter part was lest anyone might see whom Miss Roderick and the nit-nurse were indicating after the hair examination, so their identity would be anonymous to save them embarrassment, scorn and isolation. During nit epidemics, the discussion went on so long many children fell asleep and after waking went around like somnambulists for the rest of the day.

My lank hair was arranged in a complicated series of plaits with a parting in the middle. Each morning my mother would brush my hair vigorously, divide it up and, pulling it back, put two plaits on the top of my head either side of the parting, making me look as if I had nascent horns. These plaits were then incorporated into two more which hung at my back, reaching just below the shoulder. Each thin but firm little rope-like appendage ended in a splendid butterfly bow of coloured ribbon (but not yellow) — a real tempta-

167

tion for boys to dislodge, probably because the thinness of the plait exaggerated the size of the bow, making it fair game for idle hands.

Sometimes during the nit inspection hair had to be unplaited for a thorough examination and although little girls with plaits tried to help each other repair the damage done to their hair-styles, a proper adjustment of such a complicated arrangement as mine by inexperienced hands was impossible. The plait would be loose, the ribbons would drop off and get lost, then I had a load of crinkly hair getting in my eyes, obliterating my work and once finding its way into the inkwell. How I envied the girls with natural waves or curls who could keep their hair short and neat with just a quick combing. There was only one solution — have it cut short. I was so sure my mother would agree to this as I walked home one afternoon, mentally detailing the advantages of short hair and preparing my speech, that I almost made an appointment for a haircut in Lena Jaynes' hairdressing salon on the main road. However, mother was not in agreement. I was far less likely to catch nits with plaits; plaits were neat and suited me; they meant my hair had a good brushing every morning (before being tortured into ropes!); and what would we do with all the dozens of redundant ribbons?

I was so disappointed and frustrated, I called her "stupid old thing", keeping a safe distance away and preparing to be chased either out of the house or up to my bedroom by an irate mother wielding the brass toasting-fork which had on several similar occasions come forcibly into contact with my bottom and which finally disappeared, to be found many years later, mangled out of all recognition, down the side of an armchair. On this occasion I safely reached the sanctuary of my bedroom and hurriedly bolted the door behind me to cries of: "You naughty girl! Just wait till your father comes home. I'll tell him, mind, and he'll give you." This was no threat at all. Dad didn't care whether I had plaits, curls or was bald and probably wouldn't have noticed one way or the other. As for calling my mother stupid, he'd just shake his head and tell me not to do it again. He only got angry with me when I fell down when running and had bleeding knees and elbows which had to be bandaged, and developed scabs which suppurated, thus causing the lint to stick to the offending piece of raw flesh and requiring warm water, soaking and gentle persuasion to release its grip.

So really I only had Mam's wrath to contend with. I remembered one of Miss Roderick's proverbs or sayings: 'Might as well be hung for a sheep as a lamb', so took a small pair of scissors out of a vanity case, snipped off my right plait and, with its ribbon still attached, threw it out of the open window, where it landed outside the pantry near the back kitchen door.

The enormity of my action struck me on seeing the pathetic length of hair lying on the stone slab with its big red bow. I held my breath and waited. Fortunately I didn't have to wait long before I heard a door open, footsteps which suddenly stopped, a muttering of: "*Mawrth*! What on earth...?", then my mother's raised, angry voice: "Mary! What's this?"

"My plait," I bravely but tremulously replied.

"Come down here straight away."

"No."

"Come down, I say!"

"No!"

No amount of command, persuasion, inducement or finally pleading could impel me to quit my refuge until my father came to knock on my door. He had a good laugh at either my hair, my exploit or my fright, or at all three, but I was enticed downstairs by promises of his protection should my mother fly off the handle again on seeing my chopped, unbalanced hair — an intact plait on one side and uneven, spikey strands on the other, a good six inches shorter.

The damage having been done, on that occasion I finally had my way. The next morning we visited Lena Jaynes' salon, she fitted me in with an emergency appointment and I arrived at school late but triumphant with short hair.

On one occasion after the plait episode I did catch nits, although I was unaware of it at the time. The daily bathing, shampooing and scrubbing of my head might have told me something was amiss as normally this operation was once weekly on Saturday night.

There was a family called Savoury in Trehafod who like the Luckwells belied their name, as they were anything but. There were three daughters in the family who always seemed excluded from the main stream of activities and kept themselves to themselves. They were strong, quiet, fair-haired girls with large, patrician noses and names to match: Stella, Sylvia and Sonia. Their house overlooked the railway and was full of animals — dogs, cats, rabbits, and probably mice and rats too. In the garden their father kept chickens and a goat which also now and then wandered into the house. Uncle Dick's sheep sometimes took a stroll down off Gelliwion mountain to see what was going on in Trehafod and they too were made welcome in the Savoury household — in fact, potato peelings were put out to encourage them. Whatever, sheep were always hanging around in the *gwli* near the Savourys' place. Stella, Sylvia and Sonia were slow and silent but seemed very grateful if anyone took an interest in them and without saying anything would bring out their few possessions to show you: a rag doll, a dog-eared book, a lead soldier who had lost all his paint, a scruffy, one-eyed teddy bear and a home-made cricket bat split down the middle. I believe their father had no job and according to rumour their mother was *didoreth*, didn't keep the house or the daughters clean and spent a lot of time thinking.

Everyone in Trehafod knew of the Savourys but apparently few befriended them. I never ventured inside their house but once peered into the darkness inside from the back garden, and despite the door's always being open, except presumably in rain, the smell was such that even an unfussy, undiscriminating nose such as mine was offended enough to cause me to speedily withdraw, gasping for air. Mam wasn't pleased to hear I had become friendly with the Savoury girls.

"You mustn't go to their house, Mary."

I didn't tell her I'd already been and her ban was too late. "Why not?"

"Cos it's not very nice there. *Ach y fi*, they might have *bwgis*. Mrs Savoury doesn't clean. And they don't want you poking around."

"Yes, they do. They haven't got any friends 'cept me."

She tried another tack. "What about your little click of friends, Teggy Vowles and that nice Enid Morgan? They won't like it if you desert them, and the Savoury girls have got each other for company."

"Well, I like them. They're nice too."

"And they don't go to church."

"P'raps they go to chapel."

"No, they don't go there, either."

"How do you know, then?"

"Well, they're freethinkers."

170

"What's that, Mam?"

"Well, it means like... They don't believe in God."

This did rather shock me, as where would they go when they died? Not believe in God! Gracious me! At that time I was rather keen on heaven and quite looking forward to going there, as my mother had assured me that among other things you could have as much sugar in your tea as you liked, as there was no rationing in heaven.

Anyway, the upshot of my acquaintance with the Savourys was that I caught their nits and my friendship with these gentle, animal-loving if godless girls came to an abrupt end, as I was nightly kept at home to have a bath. Buckets of heated water were poured over my scrubbed head until *I* was nearly washed away, let alone the nits. Once my mother had decided on an onslaught, she was deterred by nothing and true to Winston Churchill's advice: "Never ever, ever, ever, ever give up", she never did until the cause was won. On my release from cleanliness, I was bribed with a dolls' house which had lights and tiny furniture made by my father not to go to the Savourys again.

Some months later, Mam told me I had had nits in my hair probably caught from the Savourys and I was even more horrified to think I'd had hateful little things running around my head than I was to hear Stella, Sylvia and Sonia wouldn't be coming to heaven.

After a week or so, bath night reverted to the enjoyable Saturday night ritual. Father had gone down to the Llanover Arms in Pontypridd, the shop was shut, *In Town Tonight* was on the wireless, the metal pail of water was on the fire and the tin tub in place on the mat. It was not so much the bathing I particularly liked but my affably smiling father's return from the pub with two penn'orth of chips for me and a bottle of Guinness stout. We would hear the heavy shop door opening, then my father's voice sing out in the passage: "Hello, here I am, safely home". Sometimes he would say: "Hello, my lovelies. Here I am" and my mother would look wryly at me and say: "Hmmm. Your father's well oiled tonight, Mari fach."

If I drank all the Guinness he would give me a penny because according to him it would make you strong. He, still broadly smiling, would sit down to the supper of bacon, onions and chitterling my mother had just cooked for him in a frying pan over the fire, and he would talk more than he had all week.

Once in a while in the early 'forties a strange little ceremony took place in the school assembly area. This was to assess the length of one's feet, and large enough feet qualified for supplementary clothing coupons. One's foot was placed between two lines which represented the least measure to be attained and if it spanned these two marks you had won. We were not normally told in advance of the event but children got wind of it and beforehand there was a great deal of fiddling about by the boys in the region of their boots. As socks did not have to be removed for this test, all sort of foreign bodies were introduced into them — handkerchieves, string, bits of paper which must have been very uncomfortable, cotton wool sometimes stained with ear-wax, and the occasional rubber — in order to lengthen the foot and so cross the measuring lines marked on the floor.

Girls never seemed to get up to these ruses, possibly because nothing other than feet could be concealed in white cotton ankle socks, and possibly because the competitive, winning spirit inbred in boys was missing in the fairer sex. Whereas the grey, three-quarter length sock as worn by boys could be a real treasure trove, a handy receptacle for storage for a girl, usually handkerchief and sweets, was up the leg of her knickers, though chocolate could be a bit messy, especially if you sat on it. This was useless as a purse though, the leg elastic not being tight enough to contain coins, which anyway got lost in the folds of the material. Many boys kept their money in their sock because coins jumped out of pockets as they tore around the yard, played football or hurled themselves through the air. Pockets developed holes, so money certainly wasn't safe in them. Several boys transported their exercise books in their sock, so when Miss Roderick called them up to have their homework sums marked they were warm if not all correct. Others stowed their snack for playtime in their hosiery and nibbled on soggy, curved biscuits at eleven o'clock. Other marvels that emerged from inside grey woollen stockings were sweets and soft chocolate, pencils, comics also apparently useful as shin-guards in fights or football, and the occasional frog, newt or grass-snake.

As a class we were summoned for the foot-length test and after removing shoes there was much wriggling and stretching of toes, not to mention the smoothing of strange lumps in some socks as feet strove for greater size.

172

Girls held noses and made noises of disgust if a boy in stockinged feet came near and boys nudged each other, trying to look innocent, despite apparently having a surplus provision of toes. However, no one was ever asked to remove their socks and coupons were duly distributed and proudly carried home to be handed to delighted, grateful mothers.

"Oh, there's a good boy you are, Davy John, to have big feet. With these coupons and a couple I been saving our Ginny can have a new winter coat now."

Once or twice we were summoned to the assembly area where the headmistress, standing on a small portable platform placed near a large cardboard box, said: "Now then children, you've been brought here this afternoon from your lessons as we have a special treat for you."

The first excited murmurs rippled through the classes. Was it to be a special day off? An outing? A party? Miss Lally Davies waited impatiently for silence. "Quiet. Quiet. Do you want to know what it is, or do you want to talk?"

Quiet didn't ensue as the less aware answered her question. "Yes, miss. No, miss. We want to know, miss. We don't want to talk, miss."

With her hand held aloft, her mock patient look terminated chatter. Then: "Well, as you know, the Americans are now helping Britain to win the war, and as they are very generous people — do you all know what generous is?"

There were some murmurings of "No", some shaking of heads, then a hand in the sea of expectant faces was raised, and after a nod from the headmistress: "Yes, miss. Kind, miss?"

"Good. That's right. And as the Americans are kind people and have more food than we have in our country, they have sent some of their spare supplies to the children of this country."

The eyes and mouths in the expectant faces expressed even greater delight and girls hugged themselves with anticipation. The headteacher continued: "In the education offices up the Valley last week, they received a hundred boxes like this one beside me, and today a van has been taking these boxes to all the Rhondda schools."

More speculation and excitement followed as some fully expected Father Christmas at least to pop out from inside.

"In those boxes are packets, and there is a packet for every one of you, which we will give out presently. But first we will have three cheers for the Americans and for the Rhondda Education Authority. Hip, hip..."

The hoorays were dutifully responded by the wondering pupils whose mouths were watering, imagining all sorts of delicacies in the mysterious packets.

"Now then, we don't know what's in them, do we?"

"No, miss," was the expected chorus.

"Well, now then, in those packets is — chocolate powder!"

Ooohs and aaahs were forthcoming with more hugging and hopping. The hand was raised in mock patience again.

"All right, all right. Listen. Each packet is to be taken straight home after school and you must tell your mothers to mix it with hot milk to make a hot chocolate drink, or put it in cake mix to make chocolate cake, or of course it can be eaten as it is — with a spoon."

The packets were distributed into eager hands but the last piece of advice from the headmistress as to the consumption of the chocolate powder was perhaps a little imprudent. We all knew fingers came before knives and forks, or in this case, spoons, and although the packets were obediently taken straight home as instructed, few if any arrived intact and if there might have been enough left for a weak chocolate drink there certainly wasn't enough left in any to make a chocolate cake.

CHAPTER FOURTEEN
V.E. Day

Early in May, 1945, General Montgomery accepted the surrender of the German Armies on Lüneberg Heath. Hitler had already committed suicide in his bunker and the Russians had won the race between them and the Americans to reach Berlin. I was nine years old now and for some time had been reporting back to my parents much more accurately the progress of the war from the wireless news in the Thomases'. Now that we were really winning I found that I didn't hate the Germans so much. Indeed, some months later, watching the Pathé News in the Central Cinema in Porth, where Mrs Thomas (Granny's daughter) used to take me and David, and seeing newsreel coverage of boys as young as eleven or twelve defending their homes alongside their grandads, the German equivalent of the Home Guard, I felt positive sympathy for them and even shed a few tears at the Stunde Null (Zero hour), to see homeless Berliners, their city devastated and desecrated first by Allied bombing and then by the Russians, scrounging around in waste bins and on rubbish heaps for a few scraps of food and paltry possessions.

Britain naturally went wild with celebration at the war's end — no more destruction, no more absent fathers, husbands, sons and brothers, no more hardship, no more rationing. Normality in life could resume after six years' privation and the country was going to fête this state of affairs as never before.

In fact the festivities for the day of 'Victory in Europe' celebrations and the preparations leading up to them thrilled me as nothing before in my life. Even Miss Roderick's proverb: 'It is better to travel hopefully than to arrive' didn't hold water for the arrival was equally as marvellous as the journey. Every street in the village was to be decorated, have a street party and sports. There were to be fancy dress and jazz band competitions and a procession with floats through the village with nearly everybody taking part, the whole extravaganza ending with a bonfire and dancing.

For weeks ahead sewing machines buzzed, making endless little flags and banners which were then strung at intervals on a tape intended to stretch across the width of the street from one upstairs window to a neighbour opposite. This was fine at the top end of Bryn Eirw but lower down, from 27 to us at number 40, there was nothing but a low wall opposite unimpeding our view of the valley, so tall wooden poles were erected by the menfolk to hold the flaggery and bannerage.

Everyone was in a holiday mood and good-natured local ladies on the Street Victory Committee made weekly collections around the houses of money to buy food, drink and paper hats for the street party and prizes for the various competitions and sports. Promises of help to prepare jellies, blancmanges, trifles, cakes and mountains of sandwiches were readily forthcoming, as were offers to lend crockery, cutlery and glassware, trestles, redundant doors and surplus planks for the tables.

Mothers, aunts, older sisters, grandmothers and any responsible females were press-ganged into being tailoresses to make jazz band uniforms and fancy dress costumes for youngsters. The majority were on a nationalistic theme: there were several Britannias, squadrons of tiny servicemen, mostly admirals and generals, nurses, policemen, bus conductors and chimney sweeps, one or two Winston Churchills, a minute Mr Punch and his baby sister Judy, Beefeaters, Yeomen of the Guard, Long John Silvers and a Mr Micawber. One pessimist went on parade as a convict, lugging around a ball and chain and I myself went as a Union Jack with a bowler hat — a tiring outfit as, when it mattered, I had to hold my arms outstretched, otherwise I was indeed a limp, sad flag.

The most exciting part of the whole razzmatazz was the Tump jazz band. Four or five bands had been formed in Trehafod and were busy practising for the big day — the parade and the competition to be held in the play park on the eve of the main celebrations. Anybody could be in the band provided they had a gazooka — a tin whistle type instrument, the shape of a tiny coffin, with a round, gauze-covered air-hole in the middle. You didn't need to be musically knowledgeable to play this instrument. All you had to do was hum the song and blow at the same time and a sort of tinny buzzing noise emerged vaguely resembling some tune or other. The main problem was not the music but the marching, particularly turning corners. Some children, despite hours of practice, didn't understand beating time. Others could not be persuaded to swing their arm in the opposite direction to their leg movement. Then there were others, little *twts* who had joined the band only because the evening practices gave them an excuse not to go to bed as early as usual and whose legs were too short to keep up or who were too dull to understand the drum major's signals. They dropped behind, fell over, marched constantly out of step, bumped into the quasi-musicians in front or walked on their heels, causing them to lose their shoes and hop, then slaps were exchanged and scraps followed. Finally it was decided to put them on the float as nymphs, dryads, nyads and elves with nothing to do except look decorative and with a promise of chocolate if they were good.

Besides the lines of gazooka players there was a leading bass drum, followed by four young women playing side drums at their hip. Next, on her own, came a lady with a pair of gleaming cymbals which she crashed together at what seemed to me arbitrary intervals just when she felt like it, probably as she passed someone making rude or critical comments, or a spy from another band down lower Trehafod. After her were two rows of triangle tinklers, then the rest were the gazookas and the stragglers. The person with the hardest job was the drum majorette who swung a decorated pole to right or left to tell the following marchers which street she was off to next. This young woman was a waitress in Bacchetta's café in Porth. No doubt she practised with the cups, plates and trays in her work, as soon she was demonstrating all sorts of tricks with the mace — throwing it up in a twirly manner in the air, sometimes managing to catch it as it descended, swinging it round behind her back from one hand to the other, whirling it about above her head and under her feet. It looked dangerous to me and I was glad I was safely halfway back in the band. Not everyone appreciated her display.

"Oh, tha' Moira Samuel do get on my nerves, aye. 'Ave you seen 'er throwin' that pole up in the air? Proper show-off she is."

"Aye. Oh, she thinks she's a big noise now, with that stick."

"Yeah, an' sometimes she can't catch it 'cos it goes up wonky. Tha' drummer nearly 'ad it smack in the chops last night, 'e did."

"She belongs to me, see. My mother's cousin's daughter."

"Oh, Gawd, she don', do she?"

"Yeah, but she don' come to our 'ouse now. We're not talkin' any more."

A few days before the long-awaited celebrations, the uniforms were ready. The tall red hat with white and gold braid had a white paper plume at its front and the thigh-length dresses were of the same colours with twisted gold braid loops over the chest. Footwear was white socks with white shoes or daps. The men and boys had red trousers with white side stripes. The music so improved once we donned the uniforms that it became possible to recognise the tunes played. The turns and street corners were mastered. We named ourselves 'The Tumpettes' and were ready for the contest.

Whether we won or not was immaterial and I don't remember in any case. The excitement was all: the bands (the Squadronnaires, the Legionnaires, the Majors and the Marshals) taking it in turn to parade musically around the park, eyed critically by the other contestants, loudly applauded by laughing, boisterous spectators, the noise, the colours, the crowds, the animation of the scene, the joy as the thought occasionally struck you that the nasty old war had ended.

The following day the remaining decorations were put up in the street and they hung so profusely across from every upstairs window it was not possible to see the top end of the street. It was beautiful, so gay and colourful, I had never witnessed such a spectacle in all my nine years and was considerably awed by it all. Demobbed soldiers, sailors and airmen were constantly returning home to WELCOME signs, decorated houses, hugs, neighbours' greetings and parties. Willingly and cheerily and hailed on every side, they helped put up decorations, trestles and boards for the street party tables and there was more to-ing and fro-ing than has ever been seen since: ladies laying paper table-cloths, carrying jugs of orange squash and bottles of pop, others preparing huge brown enamel pots of tea and hastening with covered plates of food, men on step ladders fixing up loudspeakers and fairy lights, manoeuvring barrels of beer and measuring out distances for the races, old men in straw hats leaning on walking canes and marvelling at the bustle, kids excitedly run-

ning round everywhere, getting in the way and underfoot, but nobody scolding or angry. In the happiness of the event, people who
had not been seen speaking to each other for years forgot their en-
mity and renewed friendships.

The party under way, children seated at one end, the elderly at the
other, wearing funny paper hats, were waited on by their mothers
and daughters, who, once these had had their fill of good things,
took their turn at the feast table.

"*Jawl* ! It's nice to 'ave a sit down and a bit of a whiff, innit? 'Ard
work, feeding the five thousand."

"Aye. *Ware teg* thcugh, 's been a lovely day, it 'ave. I won' forget
it in a 'urry."

"Yeah. Won' see nothin' like this again for a few twelvemonth."

"Good job the weather 'ave kept up. Jew, I'm thirsty, aye. I could
jes' do with a nice cup of tea now. Whass in those sandwiches over
by there, Mavis? S'not snoek, is it?"

"No, mashed tinned sardines, I think."

The tables' remaining food and litter were cleared away and loud
hailers and whistles started the street sports along the carefully
chalked out distances previously measured. Children reappeared
looking athletic in shorts and daps and ran sprints, while their older
relatives ran sack, egg-and-spoon and three-legged races, provoking
much amusement and falling about with laughter.

Finally in early evening the grand procession of the jazz bands,
led by the winners of the previous day, took place, followed by the
floats, which in turn were followed by the fancy dress parade, adults
marching smartly in time to the music, children trailing along
behind, slower and slower along Phillips Terrace and up Sant's Hill,
lengthening the winding cavalcade like a squirming worm growing
a new body. The parade assembled in the park and wended its way
up to the New Road where the floats, the little Winstons, the
Pierrots and Columbines and the multifarious pirates were ad-
judged, again to great cheering and vociferous encouragement.
There were no losers. All in fancy dress had some award to avoid
jealous juvenile fisticuffs, though some did better than others in the
prize stakes.

When dusk fell the bonfire on the lower mountain slope, a hump
silhouetted against the night sky, was lit and sparks flew energetically into the air. Shortly, fireworks, that many of the wide-eyed

young were seeing for the first time, scorched the heavens with blue and green rockets and showers of orange stars.

The show over, babies and small children were ushered home and put quickly to bed to allow their parents a night out, dancing in the streets to a wind-up pre-war gramophone with a horn. Some happy hours later, from my bedroom I heard the revels continuing into the night and fell asleep to the strains of: "What a day this has been, What a rare mood I'm in", and I couldn't have agreed more.

CHAPTER FIFTEEN
Scholarship

If most children arrived at school in the morning up to five minutes before the appointed time of arrival (some bold boys habitually put in an appearance up to twenty minutes after, of course), the majority rarely arrived back home as promptly in the afternoon. The trouble was that Trehafod was such a wonderful place for exploration. There was a lot of waste ground, a beautifully mucky, reasonably shallow and inviting river, a play park, culverts and drains for investigating, several small streams or *nants* that cried out for damming, diverting and walking in, fern-clad hillsides, God-given for hide-and-seek, railings edging roads, doubtless specially constructed for gymnastic tricks and bodily contortions, narrow, low walls and pipes for balancing on, the football field and the suspension bridge (known as 'the swing bridge') across the river at the bottom of Trehafod which required bouncing to remind it what it was for.

It was purely by hazard which route was taken back home. If the cat or dog of a friend who lived in lower Trehafod had had young, the route home, after visiting her back garden shed, would be via the swing bridge. This was a rather rickety affair built largely of wires and wooden planks. Its demise in the floods of the 'sixties must have been something of a relief to it as the construction had been so weakened by decades of children jumping and running on it and bouncing and shaking it, its hold on security was tenuous anyway. On the far side of the bridge were a few small allotments and wire-fenced areas of pig-sties, which the ear could detect long before the eye and the nose long before either. The largest of these belonged to the Chippoes who had a dozen or so sows rooting about on the sparse grass and mud bordering the river. Opposite the

Memorial Hall and in front of the Bomb and Dagger, a small building where revivalist meetings were held, the Chippoes had a general food shop which gave onto a fish and chip shop behind. Plenty of waste food was available for pig breeding — potato peelings from the chips and unsold vegetables which began rotting were all put to good use. The pig-sty was rather off the beaten track, though and to ensure the animals' safety and his continuing ownership of them, Glan Chippo had built a small shed alongside in which a man lived, paid to be the pig-caretaker.

Along the river bank above the path ran a black pipe several feet in diameter and raised up off the ground here and there up to five feet on concrete pillars built at twenty yard intervals. You could of course walk along the path invaded in places by small streams coming off the steep hillside above, but what was the point when you could walk or run along the pipe? Children who came off, grazing various limbs, could always wipe up the blood and wash the offending area in the strangely rust-coloured *nants* or, failing that, in the licorice water of the river nearby. This route involved a slippery, muddy climb up to the one-in-two gradient Parish Road, then a quick scamper across the grassy bank down which children had slide races on squares of cardboard, hanging on for dear life, below the front of the Pleasant View houses and finally into Bryn Eirw Street through the gap.

Between this gap and Terry Stores were half a dozen or so houses which seemed back to front to me, as their rear doors and yards with the tin bath hanging on the wall gave onto the street, whereas their front doors, although having a fine view across the valley, led to nowhere apart from a steep garden held in place by a high wall below which was the uneven grassy bank, the road being further down still, level with the roofs of the small terrace of Ael y Bryn. Visitors to these houses had to enter by the back door, passing the tin bath, as it was highly inconvenient for them to traipse up the soggy grassy bank, then to have to face the steep garden steps. Not only would they need sustenance, possibly even resuscitation, straight away before even the welcoming kisses and health-and-weather chat, but what if they had posh visitors, coming from Cardiff, like my god-parents, Auntie May and Uncle Ernie Causon? I was glad I didn't live in one of them.

Once in the street and within sight of home you could have a casual game of catty-and-doggy, button-flicking when no marbles were available, spinning a top, skipping or hopscotch, whichever game was in fashion, and to a mother's anxious question of: "Where've you been? You're home late today, and I was worried", you could, without any feeling of guilt, answer: "Only out in the street, playing". There was no need to mention you'd been risking your neck, running on pipes, rescuing balls from the river or crossing main roads.

The other attraction, apart from the play park behind the Trehafod Hotel with the ever-muddy metal of its slide precluding a swift descent, its rough, wooden swings which put splinters into your legs and its stiff, slow roundabout, was the football field. This was strictly out of bounds as it meant crossing the main road by the red brick urinal on the bridge, then following a narrow path, often lapped by the river and covered when it was in spate, under the dark railway bridge.

Most of the football field could be seen from the Tump and when the Trehafod team had a home game on Saturday afternoon there were as many spectators — miners in their squatting position, watching from the New Road or people resting one foot on the railings at the top of Bryn Eirw Hill opposite our shop — as there were congregated around the touchline on the field. The ground was very uneven as though the sea had washed over it and the waves solidified and while there was ample grass along the edges it was sparse down the middle and bare in front of the goals. It was a good situation for a football field as it lay between the colliery, with the railway alongside, and the river, with the Llwyncelyn road and the Cwm George waterfall beyond, so there was plenty to occupy eyes and mind when you'd had enough of the football.

Under the railway line was a high grey stone wall and if you played here you couldn't be seen from the Tump. However, forgetfulness in the enthusiasm of the game or pursuit led you from the protection of the wall, a worried father or mother would glimpse their wayward child on the football field and suddenly a name would ring out across the valley, yelled by an irate and gesticulating parent at the top of Church Hill: "Tommeee! Tommeee!" Other words followed, made incoherent by echo and distance, but Tommy would hear them quite clearly as he scrambled smartly up the hill five minutes later: "Get home this instant! Over the football field, indeed! I'll give you, you naughty boy. Straight home after school I said, didn't I?"

Sometimes the naughty child was of the opposite sex and on those days I was caught I wasn't allowed out to play after tea.

As far as we children were concerned, the only true peril on the way home from school was meeting 'Lewis the Jew' and he did put fear into young hearts. The word would go around that Lewis the Jew was abroad (but not unfortunately in the foreign sense) and children and dogs would disappear off the streets like sugared cornflakes out of a bowl.

Lewis the Jew was an itinerant tramp and appeared in the vicinity perhaps twice a year. A big man with a profuse grey beard, shaggy eyebrows and long, grey, matted hair under a battered hat, he seemed entirely clothed in flapping rags which increased the impression of size. He looked enormous to me, by far the largest person as far as height times girth goes that I had ever seen. He carried a walking stick with which, it was said, he beat the children he had stolen. Slung over his shoulder was a sack, no doubt containing his few possessions but reputed to hold the bodies of the children he had murdered on finding them unwilling or unsubservient. A frightening person indeed and one who dishearteningly appeared to be able to move fast. The problem occupied young minds.

"Will you come home with me and 'old my 'and 'cos Lewis the Jew's around?"

"Oh, I dunno. If I come home with you I'll 'ave to go the rest of the way on my own."

"You can wait in my 'ouse till my father comes 'ome and 'e'll take you to your 'ouse."

"Yeah, but then I'll 'ave a row 'cos I'm late. My mother'll think I've been over the football field."

"Aw, come on. I'm awful scared tha' Lewis the Jew might 'ave me and put me in 'is sack."

Something was usually resolved. Children, girls and boys, with abnormally fast-beating hearts, walked timorously home through the streets of Trehafod, holding hands in couples and being a perfect nuisance to other pedestrians on the pavements; then if Lewis the

Jew was espied within a hundred yards everyone would desert his friend and with much squealing run as fast as possible in the opposite direction.

One wet, stormy day when it was rumoured he was about, I got into the house as quickly as possible and was having a Marie biscuit and a glass of milk when there was a knock on the shop counter. At that time I wasn't tall enough to see above the red and yellow diamonds of the stained glass type paper covering half the pane in the top of the shop door, so simply opened it and stepped into the shop. My heart skipped several beats. When it started up again, it hammered on my chest louder than the customer had knocked on the counter, for standing before me in all his immensity was Lewis the Jew. He said something through the growth on his face but my thoughts were not on serving but on beating as hasty a retreat as possible, considering the weak state of my knees. Muttering: "I'll fetch my mother," I ran to the kitchen, telling Mam to go to the shop, and collapsed into a chair. My collapse was short-lived, however, as I thought I'd better arm myself with a broom and hover behind the shop door to ensure my mother's safety. You never knew. Although she was quite tall and solid, the tramp might put her in his sack. Some time went by. I could hear my mother talking and a gruff voice answering. Finally she emerged, looking sad.

"Oh, poor old man, tramping about in this weather. I nearly asked him in for a cup of tea and a bit of cake."

"Oh, no, Mam, you didn't."

"No, he looked so dirty, I was afraid he had fleas. So I gave him a nice glass of ginger beer instead. Perhaps that'll warm him up. All he wanted was two Woodbines."

No doubt a tramp's life is not the healthy one it is depicted as in literature, being exposed to all weathers and whims of nature. Shortly afterwards Lewis the Jew disappeared from the scene. Perhaps he frequented other haunts or shuffled off this mortal coil and gradually he faded from people's memories.

In late May the day arrived that everyone had striven for since entering the junior school — the Day of the Scholarship Exam, later to be known as the Eleven Plus, an erroneous title, since most children were ten. The whole class sat the day-long exams, but those pupils who lived on the southern side of the Trehafod Hotel did exams for the Ponty County and Mill Street schools, whereas those north of the hotel sat ⸍⸍e Porth County and Secondary schools exams.

Tense children arrived in school earlier and tidier than usual, laden with small pieces of coal, black cat brooches, dried and pressed clover leaves, Cornish pixie badges and various other lucky charms. As instructed, everyone had a clean handkerchief with them, despite its being summer and a singular absence of coughs and colds. Whether this was for tears in the event of not being able to do the sums or for mopping up ink splashes or wiping clotted nibs, no one was quite sure.

The exam proceeded as the normal school day except that the inkpots were already filled to the brim, the pens had shiny new nibs, the pencils were unused and sharpened to a pin point and there was a larger than usual square of unstained pink blotting paper on everyone's desk. Miss Roderick was very maternal with the pale-faced class before her and called everyone by their first name only.

"Leslie, have you brought a clean hanky to school today?"

"Yes, miss. Here it is, miss."

"Then blow your nose, Leslie, there's a good boy. It's running. Go on, give it a good blow. Harder than that. You don't want to be all clogged up and sniffing for the sums, do you?"

The headmistress, Miss Lally Davies, arrived with the sheaf of exam papers and, after a few cursory remarks about no cheating, trying hard and good luck, we were on our way with three-fifths times eleven-twelfths and soon into familiar territory with the trains, bath water, builders and carpets. Nibs scratched away, tongues curled around lips in concentration, hair on bent heads caressed desks. Not for twelve months since the previous exam had the room witnessed such total dedication to the task in hand. In the closing minutes answers were hastily scribbled on question papers to compare at playtime. Five minutes later I regretted that little act on discovering I had only one answer out of the twenty similar to anyone else's. Oh, crikey, I had failed already and it was only playtime... You had to pass in sums to go to the County school. What would my mother say? Perhaps I'd better not tell her I had different answers from the others.

Gritting my teeth to control the tears of disappointment and with a sick feeling in my stomach, I vowed to concentrate like mad on the mental arithmetic and went back inside saying my tables to myself.

An hour later we were presented with a choice of essay titles and for sixty minutes I wrote about My Last Birthday, relating to some unknown person in the Rhondda Education Department how the previous September I had joyfully awoken to several cards, a few parcels and presents, with the expectancy of more at my birthday tea party after school. However, the day was quite ruined as, racing home from school at mid-day to see what had arrived in the second post, I turned to look back in mid-run without pausing and forcibly collided with an iron lamp-post. splitting my head open, knocking myself out and temporarily blinding myself in my left eye. Worst of all, the birthday cards I had carried to school to show my friends and Miss Roderick were all lost, scattered in the road and run over by buses and cars and probably Mr Collins's cart. Friends led me, bleeding, partially sighted and dazed, home to my frantic mother. Dr Clarke was called. my forehead was stitched up, the party was cancelled and I spent the rest of the day in bed bemoaning my lot. As if it wasn't bad enough that my birthday fell on the second or third day of the new school year!

I chose this particular subject, rather then My Favourite Book or A Day at the Seaside, as I thought I might invoke the examiner's sympathy and he would award me a good mark to compensate for such an unfortunate birthday, which might partially make up for my disastrous performance with the assorted problems earlier in the morning.

My favourite dinner of spam and chips was ready waiting for me in the house, together with a hovering mother anxious to hear how I thought I'd done. She wasn't too happy to hear my answers were different from everyone else's and depressed me even further by saying: "Never mind, Dad'll work them out when he gets home." I set off for school again assuring her, much to her surprise, that I was "going to beat that old Cynthia Hughes".

Despite having nearly all the provisions we needed in the shop, a grocery in Porth owned by two brothers, short, silver-haired men with sparkling blue eyes and smiling faces and as identical as they possibly could be without being twins, Gwynfor and Glanmor Hughes, supplied us with goods weekly, delivered at Saturday teatime. My mother never sent an order other than a longstanding one for butter, eggs and chocolate marshmallow cakes, but left it up to the Messrs Hughes, so we never knew what would arrive. Sometimes an item of goods was dispatched which duplicated exactly what we had in our shop but nobody seemed to mind and the relationship was a friendly as well as a commercial one. However Gwynfor (or Glanmor) had a daughter, Cynthia, the same age as me, but clearly a paragon of virtue, unlike me. She was always reported as doing exactly what her parents wanted, she practised the piano for an hour every day, went to chapel uncomplaining three times every Sunday and wore a hat, did her homework as soon as she arrived home from school, never got dirty, didn't whistle or run everywhere so never grazed her knees, and wouldn't dream of telling even a small lie or disobeying her mother. Her virtues were constantly held up to me. She appeared the epitome of goodness and although I had never met her, I hated her with all my heart.

The afternoon English session passed quickly, answering questions on the young, the opposite, the collective, finishing off proverbs and comparisons and answering questions on a story. My only major blunder as far as I could remember in the afternoon session was (logically, to my mind) to call a sad play a 'saddery', 'tragedy' completely deserting my mind although the morning had been one. After all, a comic play was a 'comedy'.

After his dinner Dad settled down to his last evening tussle with problems and feeling nauseous at my lack of numerate ability I made myself scarce, wandering aimlessly around the streets, contemplating scrubbing floors in the Vaughan's Arms. A mixture of misery, boredom and hunger eventually drove me back to the house, where to my immense surprise nobody was weeping or wailing in anguish and disappointment.

"As far as I can make out you've got nearly all the answers right," my father said. "Except this one here: 10s/1d should be 10s/6d. You forgot to convert the last unit back to a sixpence, silly."

My relief was absolute and my gratitude so consummate I would have practised the piano all night and eaten all the cabbage in creation. Perhaps I had a chance of getting to one of the grammar schools after all.

Time passed and one morning, instead of shouting up the stairs: "Mary! Quarter to eight! Time to get up!", my mother came bursting into my bedroom waving a piece of yellow paper.

"Oh, Mari fach, Mari fach, you've passed for Porth County, you've passed. Twenty-fifth, it says here; twenty-fifth girl in the Rhondda," she reiterated.

We were so joyful we hardly knew what we were doing. The bacon for breakfast got burnt so I had to have shrivelled egg on toast, the cat got trodden on several times, my mother kissed the paper boy to his polite but recoiling horror, the kettle boiled over the fire causing much hissing and steamy smoke and we lost the yellow piece of paper, which sobered us up. "We haven't dreamt it, have we?" my mother kept asking, frantically looking under cushions and chairs, in jugs on the dresser and even in the tea-caddy. "Oh, I'm so excited, I don't know what I'm doing. Go to school quick, Mary, to see if they've heard there."

School indeed confirmed that two of us girls and one boy were going to be 'County Snobs' and seven or eight had passed to be 'Secondary Sardines'.

Similar numbers had succeeded in the exams for the Pontypridd schools. My mother's joy was complete when, at the weekend, lists of results were published in the *Porth Gazette* and *Rhondda Leader* and she bought half a dozen or so copies so there were spares in the event of their being mislaid like the yellow piece of paper, eventually found in the till in the shop.

Life was lived on a cloud of pink cotton wool for the next few months. Parents were proud, teachers pleased and friends were more respectful in their attitude — for a time, anyway. I could do no wrong and oddly began to enjoy practising the piano and eating my greens. My mother and I made a special trip on the bus to buy the Porth County uniform from E.R. Roberts' store of the Kingsway, Cardiff. This included a moss-green blazer with an impressive yellow badge with which I was extremely taken, containing the rather formidable school motto: *Ni wyr ni ddysg* (No knowledge without learning).

One morning an invitation arrived in the post to go to tea and meet Cynthia Hughes who lived in Porth and who had also (naturally) passed for the County School. I wasn't too keen on this but didn't argue or complain to spoil the delightful dream I was living. Anyway I was curious to see this model of excellence, so the kind invitation was accepted.

Of course, contrary to all expectations, Cynthia turned out to be a perfectly normal girl, not as much of a tomboy as me but certainly not a goody-goody. I am sure I detected a streak of mischief waiting to develop. Her mother was a warm, welcoming person who had no airs or graces despite having the swankiest house I'd ever been in, with a toilet downstairs *and* a bathroom upstairs. We had a memorable tea with salmon sandwiches, chocolate marshmallow cakes which Glanmor (or Gwynfor) knew I liked, trifle, and no compulsory plain bread and butter. It was a very enjoyable afternoon exploring the attic, playing board games, tinkling on the piano and playing hide-and-seek all over the house. Cynthia did indeed play the piano well and years later, sadly after her mother had died, took a B. Mus at Aberystwyth.

So one era was ending and another beginning. New friends, new surroundings, and a new way of life. Perhaps they will be recorded one day.

Afterthoughts

Alas, Trehafod has changed and I have gone away, but with an incomplete heart. Part of it will always remain there; it draws me back from time to time. Some of my relatives have had the good sense to remain, so Trehafod still nourishes our roots, albeit not as flourishing as before.

Coedcae and the lower ponds have been drained and flattened and mountain water runs down to the river in no-nonsense fashion via pipes and conduits. No sheep graze Gelliwion mountain now, as it is covered in pine and fir trees, and, while it still shelters the Tump, the shadow it casts is dark and silent.

The three-quarters of a century old shop was reconverted back to a house many years ago; the bakehouse is now a bathroom. Cars line the street where children ran freely, played catty-and-doggy, cricket, release and rounders. Now it is too dangerous. A main arterial road by-passes Trehafod, cutting a swathe between the colliery and the football field, which now has rugby posts, though the trusty buses still toil up Sant's Hill, but far less frequently. The stop is still called the Vaughan's Arms, though sadly Andrew Vaughan and his pub have long gone. There are houses for sale in all the streets; television aerials like wagging fingers bestride their roofs and satellite dishes hug their walls.

The Lewis Merthyr colliery hooters no longer disturb the peace in their reassuring fashion. Colliers do not call at Cobner's for their Woodbines, but sit redundant in the club, talking about the old days. They do not knock each other up in the early daylight hours and the tramp of hobnail boots no longer echoes on road and pavement. All the tips are green and there are no trams creating more. The Rhondda river runs clear all year long; it has no secrets now. The colliery is clean and spick and span, and children may enter its grounds to roam on payment of an admission fee. Its

191

colliers are static, frozen in time, the last museum representatives of mining in the Rhondda.

The church bell tolls and calls the faithful, but a new hand pulls the rope. Its walls mourn for its most faithful ever servant, Emlyn, now confined to his home but whose spirit no doubt will forever walk the aisles at night, collecting the offertory in his verger's robes.

Milk is sold in bottles or bought in litre cartons, and vinegar is no longer delivered in barrels by horse and cart. Candles are not needed and block salt not made.

There is a play park for Tump children, since wandering on the mountain is dangerous in these days of unemployment, high inflation, poll tax, high interest rates and enforced leisure when the media of the 'nineties teach man to be unnatural.

Hafod school still functions, though less happily I think than before. Teachers are constrained, unappreciated and harassed by constantly changing governmental demands on their time and energies and children are disrespectful.

Are there characters like those of former days around? I hope there are, or village life is that much poorer. But time passes, life evolves, manners and even principles in these times change. Many scoff at the past, but for me, Trehafod, Rhondda, when I was young? They *were* the good old days.